WHEN THE CAPE COMES OFF

TAMEKA FARRIÉR

VMH ™ Publishing
3355 Lenox Rd. NE Suite 750
Atlanta, GA 30326
www.vmhpublishing.com

Hardback ISBN: 979-8-9853349-0-6

Paperback ISBN: 979-8-9853349-1-3

Ebook ISBN: 979-8-9853349-2-0

Library of Congress Control Number
Available Upon Request

Published in United States of America

10 9 8 7 6 5 4 3 2 1

WHEN THE CAPE COMES OFF

A Memoir by

TAMEKA FARRIÉR

Preface

I CAN SIT HERE AND tell you my life is no different than anyone else's but that would be a lie. My life is not better than anyone else's, nor is it worse than anyone else's but one thing is for sure: my life is different than most. I have always been different as it pertains to my personality, character, and flaws, or how I handle certain people and situations, but I haven't met anyone who has been through what I have.

Throughout my life, I've had good times, hard times, triumphs, and struggles just like anyone else, but I've also had hand-ups and stepping stones. No matter what I was going through or dealing with, I've always put other's needs before my own. If they needed the fighter, I was there. If they needed the bold, outspoken person, I was ready. If they needed the funny, crazy life of the party, that was me too. I was there when my friends and family needed comfort. When my friend's mother was murdered, I was there. When another friend found out her boyfriend was cheating on her, I was there. When another friend lost her baby, I was there. When people needed advice and guidance, I was there. I was the backbone, the strong one. I never minded because I knew I could handle that pressure.

I was the peacemaker, the motivator, the pusher. It didn't mean I had everything together. It just meant I was great at balancing my struggles and helping others with theirs. I was young but I had experienced many trials growing up, which made it easy for me to relate to people. At a young age, I was filled with more wisdom than my peers. People trusted me; I was the problem solver and they felt comfortable talking to me. I had a way of making people feel comfortable by not judging them and simply listening and encouraging them. I genuinely wanted to help people and often, those were the exact type of people I attracted.

But what happens when the tables turn, and I need to be pushed and motivated? Who was in my corner? Who could I turn to? Who could I trust to keep my deepest darkest secrets without judging me? What happens when I need guidance but have no one who could relate? Here I was in search of someone to give me what I was putting out all these years, and I couldn't find it. I was surrounded by people but I knew that the people closest to me would not be able to help me. My entire world was turned upside down in the blink of an eye and I felt so alone. I was dying inside, and no one cared enough to reach out to help me.

"Do they not see me?" I thought.

"Are they hearing me?" I said to myself. How do I even ask for help from the same people who depended on me?

One day I was a young wife married to a hard-working semi-pro football player and mother of two young boys and a daughter, and the next, I became a 24 hour a day, 7 days a week caregiver for my husband who was diagnosed with heart and kidney failure, to my eldest son who was diagnosed with severe ADHD, and to my baby boy who was born with Down Syndrome and Autism. I knew people who had kidney failure. I knew other people who had children or siblings with ADHD. I even knew someone whose cousin had Down Syndrome, but I never knew anyone who carried the full responsibility of caring for all these very different diagnoses simultaneously. I had to wake up every day knowing my life would never be the same, and I had absolutely no one to turn to or vent to without judgment. What do you do, when you have all of this going on and only yourself to turn to? What happens when the cape comes off

My name is Tameka Farriér and this is my story.

Contents

CHAPTER 1

In The Beginning

WHEN I MET MY HUSBAND, he played football for a local semi-pro team in Richmond, California. He weighed 250lbs and stood at 6'4. Tall, dark, and handsome were the first three words that came to mind when I first met him that cool, spring evening at the club. I was there with my girlfriend, against my will. To my surprise, when we arrived at the club we were greeted by my cousin and her husband on the dance floor. We were talking, dancing, and I was finally starting to have a good time. Then, I saw him. This tall, big, sexy, chocolate man walked up to my cousin's husband; they dapped and started talking.

I grabbed my cousin and said, "Girl, who is that?"

Without hesitation she grabbed me and we walked closer to her husband and sexy chocolate, and she interrupted their conversation.

"Excuse me. My cousin wants to meet you!"

She was quick, I didn't have time to be embarrassed or shy! I just stood there and extended my hand. He smiled. I smiled back, then my cousin's husband introduced us right away.

"Karl, this is Tameka."

"Nice to meet you," I said as I was shaking his hand like we were making a business deal.

"You too," he said smiling. "You wanna dance?"

I looked him up and down because in my head I was saying "hell yeah!"

But I had to play it cool, so I simply said "sure."

We immediately started dancing and vibing with each other. The night felt so young. The DJ played all the best songs and we didn't miss a beat. After several songs, I thanked him and told him I would catch him around. I really wanted to dance with him all night, but I couldn't let him know that. We eyed one another the rest of the night.

Eventually, we snuck off to a small bar area to talk. I asked him if he had a girlfriend. He didn't. He asked me if I had a boyfriend. That was no for me as well. We asked the basic questions, "Where are you from?

Where do you live" etc. He didn't live far and seemed to be nice, so I hit him with a quick memorable line, I said "Don't leave this club without getting my phone number." Then I walked away.

I didn't know who I thought I was when I hit him with that line, but I sure did, just like that. Before the club closed, there he was to get my number. After that we talked every night; then every night turned into every day. I couldn't wait to hear from him. There was something different about him. I couldn't put my finger on it, but I fell, and I fell fast. We started dating and hanging out, and he was a real gentleman always opening doors and buying flowers or candy. I attended a few of his football games. I even brought some friends along to check him out. Some nights, when he was at work, I would get up and drive an hour to spend his 30-minute lunch breaks with him. I felt safe, and he made me feel good. He always complimented me and smiled at me. No man had ever made me blush the way he did.

He always showed me respect, love, and compassion. We quickly fell in love and moved in together after dating for a month and a half. Initially, we thought it would be good for Karl to move in with me at my cousin's, but we quickly learned we needed our own place. At the time, he was living with his baby's mother, Felicia, who was still living with her mother, sister, niece, and a slew of other relatives. Before the judgment comes, they were not together, and Karl made it perfectly clear to me. They had a three-year-old daughter, and he adored her, but the love he once had for Felicia had long faded away. She still had feelings for him and had a hard time accepting the fact that he was moving on. At first, I felt sorry for her, but then Felicia attempted to cause issues between Karl and me and even went as far as stopping him from seeing their daughter.

We had conversations about his living situation. He had a job and owned his car, but he was also giving Felicia most of his money, making it impossible for him to save enough money to move. I challenged him with difficult questions about moving out if he had the opportunity. I wanted to gauge him to see if he was lying to me, playing games, or really stuck in a bad situation.

He had been living in an apartment with a roommate prior to meeting Felicia until one day their place got robbed and left them with nothing. Growing up in foster care, Karl had no family or friends to turn to for help and ended up living in a homeless shelter. Still getting up and going to work every day, he was desperate for a new start which is when he met Felicia.

They had met through her sister one day while taking the train and they had become good friends. Shortly after their introduction, her grandmother became ill and they needed someone to come help take care of her, which presented Karl an opportunity to move out of the shelter and into their house and he did.

Although they weren't a couple, Karl and Felicia got into a sexual relationship and, after a couple of years, Felicia became pregnant. After their daughter was born, her grandmother passed away. With her grandmother gone, underlying issues arose between Karl and Felicia and the relationship became toxic. Someone was going to end up dead, in jail, or both. It was so bad one time he confided in me that he tried to take his own life by swallowing a ton of prescription pills one day in the bathtub. He was ready to die; he couldn't take it anymore and anything would be better than where he was and what he was going through. He said he cried out to God and just prayed for help right before swallowing the pills, hoping his worries would end. Well, God answered his prayers because, not long after, his Felicia and her family ended up finding him locked in the bathroom unresponsive. Their uncle had to break the door open and that's where they found him passed out. They ended up calling 911 and frantically waiting for the ambulance. He was still breathing when they arrived, and they took him to a nearby hospital where he was conscious but very weak. He survived that attempt and didn't know whether to be sad or grateful, but he knew something had to change.

He was afraid to leave Felicia's house because he felt stuck. He knew they were simply co-parenting, but in his child's mother's eyes, he lived there so she was in control and whatever she said, went. He was in love with his daughter, although I am sure they were still having sex, in his eyes, it was over. He loved his daughter but couldn't stand her mother at that time, but he needed a place to stay, and I believed him. I really liked him and after hearing all the drama between them, listening to how he grew up and what had happened to him I felt bad for him, and so I never doubted what he told me.

Although I was living with someone else, I still found myself stepping into the role of helper and offering Karl a place to live if he really wanted to get out of his situation. Imagine to my surprise a couple of weeks later when I received a phone call around 11:00 pm from Karl's sister, Joi. When I answered, I heard Joi screaming in the background.

"If you touch his car with that knife, I am gone fuck you up!" I heard Joi yell.

She yelled to Felicia's mother "Come get her!

I sat on the phone in disbelief and asked, "What the hell is going on?"

"Did you mean what you said when you told my brother that he could come live with you?"

She was out of breath because she was trying to fight off Felicia who kept trying to stab Karl's tires because he was packing up his stuff.

"Yes," I said without hesitation. "Do I need to come up there?"

I didn't even wait for an answer. I was already getting dressed. It wasn't exactly around the corner, but I didn't care, I was going to get my man! I got to San Francisco, where they had lived, in about 40 minutes, I was flying down that highway. On my way there, I kept thinking that girl was crazy, and I must be crazier because it was after midnight and I was doing 100 on the freeway to go get a man who, I honestly barely even know. But everything in my heart was telling me to go, and I did.

I met Karl and Joi around the corner from Felicia's. They were sitting in his car with everything he owned. It was so full they had to put some items in my car. I walked up to him, and he looked so defeated, hurt, and nervous. It hurt my feelings to see him look so defeated, and I know he was afraid because he was taking a big risk by leaving his daughter and starting over. The last thing he wanted was to start a new relationship just to have it end and be homeless or worse. I walked over to him, gave him a big hug, and tried my best to assure him that I was going to be there for him. I told him this was not going to be another situation, and that I really cared about him. I promised him I would help him, and he would never have to go back to that house, nor would I ever put him through what he just experienced. That is how we ended up moving in together.

CHAPTER 2

New Life

LIVING WITH MY COUSIN AND her family didn't last long. I always knew it was difficult when you lived with other people, but I had no idea it would cost me a relationship. My cousin's husband, Derick, had a problem with Karl living in the house with us. Even though he was working, treated me well and we cooked and cleaned, it was always tense for no reason. Looking back, I think it was a territorial thing. Just like lions in the safari, there can only be one male in a pride and, if any other male tried to enter, a fight would ensue. Someone had to go.

Karl and I would often go to my parents' house for the weekend and return to Hayward during the week. My parents lived in a small suburb called Pittsburg which was an hour north of Hayward. One weekend we returned to Hayward to find the locks changed.

I immediately called Serena and asked her what was going on and she told us that Derick wanted to talk to us. They were out and she insisted we wait until they arrived before we went back into the house. I didn't understand why they locked all our belongings in the house nor why they needed to talk to us. That was the last straw for us. We weren't going to sit around and wait for them, we paid rent there and they had no right to lock us out. We decided enough was enough and we were leaving that day. We walked around to the back of the house and Karl helped me get inside by removing a screen from the window. Once I was inside the house I walked to the front, opened the door, and let Karl in.

We immediately started packing all our belongings, unsure where we were going. We just knew we were leaving and loaded whatever would fit into our cars.

"We will get new stuff," I said. "Let's just get out of here."

We were pulling out of the driveway when Serena and Derick pulled up beside us. Karl was behind me in his car and because I stopped of course he stopped also.

Serena said, "We need to talk, let's just go sit down and talk."

Before I could respond, Derick ran over to Karl's car, snatched the keys out of the ignition, and sucker-punched him through the rolled-down window. Karl immediately jumped out of the car and they began to fight. Serena was screaming at Derick to stop as the men made circles in the middle of the street. It was a hot summer day around 2 pm in the afternoon and tensions were high. Surprisingly, none of the neighbors came out to see what was going on and I was glad they didn't because I didn't want the police to be called. I quickly jumped out of the car without thinking and ran over to the guys. Karl was telling Derick to give him his keys. Derick was more upset that we broke into the house more than anything and he kept blaming Karl for it. Mid swing, as Derick tried to hit Karl but missed, I was able to jump in front of him, and then I walked closer to Derick and pushed him. Now I am 5'9 and then I was about 200 lbs. so I wasn't a small girl, but Derick was about 6'2 weighing about 350. He was a street dude. He grew up in the streets, he was known for his temper and killer ways but none of that mattered to me. I was in love and, more importantly, I was angry! As I pushed him, I yelled at him to give us our keys so that we can go.

I told him, "If you want to be mad and hit someone, hit ME! I'm the one who told him to open the window so we can get our stuff!"

I was so hot, I was seeing red, and I think he knew I must have been crazy or just stupid to jump in between two men fighting and defend Karl. I pushed him again and yelled at him to give me Karl's keys. He stopped dead in his tracks and was just glaring at me. He had his hands up in the air and I was able to snatch the keys from his hand without any struggle. I could tell he didn't want to hit me, but I wasn't backing down. He let me take the keys from his hand, and I turned around telling Karl to get in the car as I tossed him the keys. Serena ran towards Derick, who was still standing there in shock. I opened my car door, put my car in drive, and looked out the window one last time because I knew we would never be back, and we drove off.

It was a quiet hour long drive back to my parents' house. I just kept replaying what happened in my head over and over wondering what we were even fighting about? How did we end up going through that and why? As we pulled up to my parents' house, I jumped out the car and said, "Karl I'm so sorry he hit you and I'm so mad.

He looked up at me, and asked "Why did you stop?"

"I don't know," I kept saying apologetically, "but I am so sorry."

As if things couldn't get any worse, I had to convince my parents to allow me to move back home which was not difficult, but to also allow my boyfriend to move in with us.

Six months passed and we experienced every hardship known to man. It was difficult living with my parents but that is to be expected when you are an adult living at home. We were 25 and 26 years old at that time and we needed a restart with our lives. Although our parents were kind enough to allow us to live there, we knew it would be temporary. My parents were always known for being the "cool" parents, meaning they weren't strict, but everyone, including myself, was surprised they allowed my boyfriend to not only live in the same house with us, but allowed us to share the same room.

My mother and Karl had several run-ins because she couldn't understand why I was so in love with this man. I never really brought men home like that before, and this man was different because he had a child and a whole lot of baby mama drama. They bumped heads because she didn't understand him and he didn't understand her. My dad was the neutral party, so he was always able to smooth things over. It got so bad one time that Karl said he was leaving and so I started packing our stuff and told him I was leaving too. He tried to convince me to stay with my family, but I felt I'd sacrificed already and we loved each other so, if he didn't feel comfortable, I didn't either. Once my mother saw how serious I was about Karl, she finally let her guard down and they had a very long conversation of understanding. Karl wasn't used to rules, he wasn't used to structure nor our family dynamic. So, when my mother would say things to us, he would take offense to it, even though she was right. It was her delivery that didn't sit well with him. They were able to hash out all their feelings and after hours of tears, arguments, and discussions they both came out of the conversation waving their white flags. We knew our living situation was temporary, we just had to get back on our feet and figure out our plan.

Karl was still playing football but his focus had drastically shifted. He had been through a slew of jobs since moving in with my parents. The drive to his job was now an hour and a half away from where we lived. It was too far and not worth the money, so he resigned, and couldn't find anything stable in close proximity. During that time, we were back and forth in court because Felicia wouldn't allow him to see their daughter. It was a very stressful situation for the both of us, but we were in it together. I was working two jobs to make sure we had everything we needed while we were looking for a place of our own and Karl continued looking for employment. All of this, compounded with child support, took a toll on us financially, but I never allowed that to slow us down.

It wasn't long before we finally found our own apartment which was not too far from my parents'. We were able to get back on track! Karl had found a steady full-time job, I continued to work, we had everything we needed, but most importantly, we had each other. Before we knew it, a year had passed, Karl was paying child support, our rent was always paid on time. We didn't have much but it was working, and life began to look up until one November day I realized I was late.

#IAMBRAVE

CHAPTER 3

Fast Track

I'LL NEVER FORGET THE DAY I walked into our apartment. It was December and it was cold outside. I walked up the stairs, opened the door and sat on the armrest of the couch, taking off my coat. Karl was home, he didn't have to be at work until later that evening.

With eyes locked on the video game, he said, "Hey Boo, what's up? How was your day?"

He never called me by my name. I was always "Boo," and when he did say my name, I always felt like I was in trouble.

I took a deep breath, put my chin up and said, "We need to talk."

He immediately froze, paused his game, sat back on the couch, and just looked at me. He didn't know what was about to come out of my mouth; he appeared to be afraid.

"I'm pregnant," I said.

He just looked at me. We'd discussed kids and marriage often, and I was adamant about not having kids. I was the eldest of four and had to carry a lot of responsibilities all my life. Plus, California was and still is an awfully expensive state for two young people, let alone a baby.

"Are you serious?" He asked me.

"Yes," I said.

I'd just gotten back home from the doctor's office to confirm.

"Okay." He said as he took a deep breath.

He didn't seem angry, but he wasn't happy either. He was trying to process what I'd just said. I was shocked and numb. There was no overwhelming joy, just waves of numbness and trying to come up with a plan. A few weeks later we made the announcement to my family because we'd decided to keep the baby. My mother owned a daycare and my sister worked for her full time, so I thought to myself "Well at least we don't have to pay for childcare."

Boy, was I wrong.

Karl and I were in the kitchen of my parents' house with my parents and baby sister, my other sister was in the living room. My mother was at the kitchen table working on her computer, and my dad was packing his lunch for work. I didn't know how they would react because my sister, who was six years younger than I, just had a baby nine months before I found out I was pregnant.

I said, "We have some news," and everyone immediately looked at me as I sat across the table from my mom and Karl stood behind me.

"I'm pregnant," I said, with a straight face.

My sisters immediately started smiling, and my youngest sister who's twelve years younger than me said, "Fa real?"

"Yes, I'm due in August."

My mother stared at me for about three minutes before speaking. Even though I was twenty-eight years old, paying my own bills and rent, I was still fearful of my mom in a way.

"Well, I don't know who is going to watch him because daycare is expensive," she blurted out, and continued typing on her computer. I wasn't prepared for her reaction.

"You can watch my baby, like you do my niece" I said with a slight attitude.

Out of all the things she could've said to me, that is what she said. No congratulations, no nothing, just "who is watching your baby?"

"Your sister works for me, so she watches her own baby!" She snapped back at me.

"Okay Mom." I said, not wanting to argue. "I just wanted you all to know. I will figure it out."

Karl didn't say a word the entire time. He learned from my father to be seen and not heard when the women were talking and things got heated.

"Let's go, Karl," I said as I stood up to push my chair in.

"Well congratulations!" My sisters said as they seemed happier for me than my mother.

"Thanks," I said. "I'll call you all later."

My mother was a very strong woman. She raised us to be strong and independent. She never took "no" for an answer and she was always ready to fight, literally. She was highly intelligent, and she could've been an attorney but as life would have it, she had kids and started her own business. My mother raised us with tough love. My brother and my two sisters are all quite different but the one thing we all shared was tough love. My mom was far from a Claire Huxtable. She rarely showed emotions or affection, and I didn't realize just how much that impacted me until way later. I didn't hate her for it because at the end of the day I knew she loved us but had a funny way of showing us love, and most of the time it was surrounded by money. Because my mother worked hard, married my stepdad, moved us from the hood and into the suburbs, I respected her hustle and how hard she worked. My mother wasn't afraid of anyone or anything. Nothing was going to stop her from living her life the way she wanted.

My first pregnancy wasn't bad, but I was huge, gained seventy pounds. I was always hungry and ready to sleep at any given moment. It didn't take long for my mother to finally adjust to the fact that her first baby was having a baby. She started to become more and more excited. Things started to look smooth again for us, that is until my husband proposed to me. My family was not as excited at first because they felt like he did it out of order. He didn't ask my mom or my dad for my hand in marriage. Instead, he and his mentors went to pick out a ring, took me out to dinner, and he popped the question on one knee right there in the middle of the Cheesecake factory in Walnut Creek, California. Everyone inside the restaurant watched in awe as he asked me to marry him.

"Of course!" I said happily as he slid the ring on my swollen finger.

We broke the news to my family after the fact in which they weren't too thrilled but were in fact happy that we wanted to get married.

Karl and I went back and forth over when to get married. I wanted to rush it seeing as how I was already four and a half months pregnant.

"We live together, I am carrying your son, there's nothing else left to do but get married." I would plead with him.

I was dead set on not being a "Baby Momma," but Karl on the other hand felt indifferent. It was almost like he was getting cold feet before the wedding even started. We often had arguments about it because I felt like now is more time for us to exchange vows, but Karl felt like I was rushing him. I would get so upset with him because I didn't understand why he would ask me to marry him, but not want to get married. There's nothing wrong with being a baby momma; I just didn't want to be one, especially after having been through so much drama with his child's mother, so I was dead set on getting married. One day he made me so mad when he told me that I was peer pressuring him that I just threw up my hands and said forget it. I don't want to get married anymore because I was sick of his reactions when I brought it up. Blame it on the hormones, but I didn't care about having a big fancy wedding, paying thousands of dollars we didn't have to entertain people who really didn't even matter, we were the ones saying "I do". I was ready to waddle my big pregnant self in front of the judge and exchange our vows in front of two witnesses and call it a day! But I left the subject alone.

Then a few months later when we woke up one morning Karl suggested that we head to the courthouse and get married.

"Right now?" I said excitedly. "Don't play with me."

It was a hot Wednesday morning in July. I was 8 months pregnant, I could barely fit in anything, let alone a wedding dress, but I didn't even care. I was so shocked he was down to go.

He said, "Let's do it!" We called his mentors. Again, I didn't even tell my family. I just threw on the first white summer dress that I could find, and we hopped in the car and drove straight to the courthouse. I didn't tell my family because I didn't want them trying to control my day or make me upset by saying something unsupportive. I just said we would tell them after it was done. We paid for our marriage license, our witnesses waited with us for the judge and, within an hour, we were married.

#IAMLOVED

CHAPTER 4

A Part of The Plan

ONE THING I KNOW IS being pregnant in the summertime was tough, but I was able to eat and do whatever I wanted, and people were so nice to me, including my mom. She became really excited about being a grandmother again. Everyone was happy and I believe it was because we found out we were having a boy. Karl was very happy about having a son and things started looking up again, but not everyone was as happy as we were.

Karl's baby mother found out through their daughter that I was expecting, and she was livid. Prior to that, she was being kind and following the court order, allowing her daughter to come visit us, but after hearing that news, she quickly slid back into her old ways and stopped allowing his daughter to come over our house even though we had a court order. Felicia cared nothing about that court order. She was still in love with Karl so she did anything and everything she could to try and hurt him, but I was right there with him, supporting him and fighting fire with fire assuring him that one day she would calm down but until then, we will let the courts handle her. I didn't want to be stressed out about anything because my son was due any day, and I wasn't going to allow anyone to make me upset as I prepared to bring a child into the world.

On August 25, 2010, I gave birth to a healthy 7lb 5oz baby boy, and he was such an angel. He had these beautiful brown eyes, a head full of curly hair. I don't know where he got his complexion from, however, he looked bi-racial because his skin was so light, but nonetheless he was ours and we were grateful. My husband was ecstatic to have a son, someone to carry his name, someone to do boy things with. He was going to be just like his daddy in every way, especially since he was born six days before his birthday. Funnily enough, he was due on my husband's birthday but came a few days early. We named him Khalil Sebastian, and he was loved by my entire family, and he had everything an only child could ever want. It seemed like time was flying by and life was good to us, maybe too good to us. I don't know if something was in the water or what because the day Khalil turned ten months old, we found out we were pregnant again!

I had so many emotions and feelings running through me, I wasn't happy or sad. I was just present. I couldn't believe I got pregnant again so fast. I didn't know when it happened because I didn't missed a period until after I found out. The doctor told me that it takes a while for a woman's body to return to normal after childbirth, but what I did not realize was how fertile a woman is after having a baby. I wasn't excited like I was with my first pregnancy, and truth be told, I was still adjusting to being a new mother and a wife. I was balancing working full-time, having a new baby, having to keep a house clean, dinner cooked and groceries in the house all while keeping my son from putting things in his mouth, changing diapers, feeding him all off five hours of sleep a night. Now here I am, pregnant again. Karl was just as shocked as I was, and don't get me wrong, we knew how I got pregnant, the shock for us was we weren't expecting to be pregnant so soon. Of course, my mother was not happy at all although she fell in love with my first son, she knew we were struggling, and she kept reminding me how much more difficult it was going to be once our second child was born. I quickly fell into depression thinking about what life would be like with two kids under two.

We were making it, but barely. I started to have panic attacks, I could not sleep, my mind was always racing then I was diagnosed with Postpartum depression.

Postpartum depression is very common among new mothers. It's an imbalance of the chemicals in your brain, and its functions because, technically, your body has been through trauma. Not only does your life change, but most new moms also don't get adequate rest, we are worrying about the baby, are they breathing? Are they eating enough? Are they sleeping enough? And we tend to function off fumes and that wreaks havoc on our bodies. The doctor offered me some medication for it, but I did not take it. I was not big on taking medicine and especially ones that basically numb you. I felt this was something I could handle, and I will figure it out on my own. I was so confused on what to do. I even spoke to Karl about not keeping the baby. He ultimately said that choice was up to me, but he felt as though we had been through a lot already, there was nothing we could not handle. I numbed myself from thinking about it for a while because I was driving myself crazy. Time must have flashed by like lightning because, before I knew it, I was already five months pregnant, so I did not have a choice on an abortion anymore, we were having this baby, and I finally accepted it. There was no way I was going to endure nine months of pregnancy, and hours of labor just to give my baby to someone else and besides, my family, although questioning my decisions, would never allow me to give up my child. I had to accept the fact that I was going to be a mother of two under two and just like the first one, this one was a boy also.

I felt so detached with this pregnancy, it wasn't like my first pregnancy at all. I couldn't allow myself to get happy. It was more like a "it is what it is" type of deal. I didn't want a baby shower. I wouldn't let people touch my belly, barely wanted to leave the house, and I just couldn't get a grip. I didn't even have a name for this baby, so I let my baby sister name him, and she called him Kayden. Karl decided to give him his middle name and he called him Emmanuel. I asked him where he got that name from, and he said it means "God with us". I don't know what changed, or what happened, immediately after Karl gave him his middle name, a light bulb went off. I remembered God has been with us, and he has helped us, and he will continue to help us. We weren't super religious, but we did believe in God and knew he was real. I finally started to feel like I was pregnant. I was getting my happy back, and I was getting prepared to bring this second baby into the world. I had some health issues during this pregnancy that required me to go to visit the doctor more frequently. I was diagnosed with something called Placenta Previa, which simply meant my uterus was covering my cervix. I was going to have a scheduled c-section which was fine with me especially since I ended up having to have one with my last son. During the birth of my first son, when I was in labor, the cord wrapped itself around my son's neck causing us to have an emergency c-section. At least with the second pregnancy, we could plan ahead for my c-section, or so we thought. Just when things started to go back to normal, we were hit by reality, and we were hit hard.

#IAMWORTHY

CHAPTER 5

A Moment I Would Never Forget

BECAUSE OF MY PREGNANCY CONDITION we knew that we were going to have a planned c-section. I was about seven months and two weeks pregnant when I was going to the doctor weekly for checkups. I was still working full-time, rearing a very busy one-year-old and managing being a new wife. One cold day in March on the 2nd, we had a doctor's appointment. Like normal they took ultrasounds, we waited for the results then proceeded to speak with the doctor. Everything looked good, everything seemed normal, so they scheduled my next appointment, and we left the hospital. As we were walking back to the parking lot of the hospital, trying to decide what to eat, my cell phone rang. It was my doctor.

"Hello," I said anxiously. "This can't be good."

He asked me if we were still in the parking lot, and I told him we were. He asked us if we could come back upstairs, that he needed to talk with us and of course we obliged.

We started walking back towards the hospital and I looked at Karl and said, "Something is wrong."

"Don't say that," Karl said. "It could be nothing."

A thousand thoughts were running through my mind. I felt something in my heart. There's no way this can be good.

As we walked back into my doctor's office, he slowly opened the door and I anxiously asked him "What's wrong?"

He asked me to have a seat, looked at Karl, then me and said, "I'm sorry but there's something wrong with the baby."

I asked, "What do you mean?"

"Something is wrong with his heart, and it looks like something is wrong with his intestines, but I can't really see that well on my ultrasound machine. I made you an appointment on Monday to go see the specialist.

"What!?" I said in shock. "What do you mean?"

He said he wasn't sure because he couldn't get a clear picture but assured me that, on Monday, we would find out everything. It was Friday. "So, we have to wait all this weekend in agony knowing something is wrong and you all don't even know?" I said angrily.

"It's okay," Karl said to me as he grabbed my hand trying to calm me down.

If it's one thing Karl can attest to while I was pregnant, it was my mood going from 0 to 100 in five seconds, so he always tried to keep me as calm as possible.

"Everything will be okay." The doctor said, "we just need to be sure what is going on. I am sending you there as a precaution."

The weekend felt like it was dragging. I couldn't sleep or eat. I was so worried. No expecting parents wanted to hear those words. How was I supposed to relax knowing that something was wrong? I had to wait two days before I could find out what was wrong.

I remember praying the entire weekend and saying "God, whatever it is, please let my baby be okay".

Monday we were at the specialist office bright and early. We went into this huge, cold room where they spent an hour and a half taking all kinds of pictures of the baby. I was so nervous I almost threw up. Karl was sitting right by my side the entire time. I couldn't tell from the technician's face if things were good or bad because her facial expression never changed. She explained to me what she was doing and that after her findings she would share with the doctor, and then the doctor would come speak with us. It was the longest hour and a half of my life. I was so scared. Karl and I just sat in silence unaware of anything. Finally, about 30 minutes after the technician was finished, the doctor came into the room and all eyes were on her. She pulled up a chair and had a file with a lot of paperwork in her hand. I looked at Karl who looked just as nervous as I was.

"Your baby has a heart defect called A-Ventricular Heart Defect, and he is going to need surgery right away after he is born. He also has another defect called Duo Duodenal Atresia which is a rotation of the intestines, and he is also going to need surgery to repair those right away, and because he has these two defects, we strongly think your son has Trisomy 21 which is also known as Down Syndrome."

The doctor kept talking, but I couldn't hear anything else she said. Her lips were moving, but I was thinking and processing what she just said to me. I looked over to Karl who looked like a deer in headlights. I knew this was real. I can't remember what I was thinking. All I knew was my baby was not okay.

By the time I tuned back the only thing I heard was, "Your baby is too big for late term abortion in the United States, but you can go to Mexico where they perform them there. Here is some information about that." She handed me a pamphlet on late term abortion.

I snapped out of my trance when I heard that. "Mexico?" I said abruptly, still trying to piece together what just happened.

"How can I go to Mexico?" I asked still in shock. "I am 7 ½ months pregnant! I am having a boy! My sister already named him, and you want me to go to Mexico to have an abortion? He has a name!"

"By law I am required to give you these options. It's completely up to you." She stated. "I am going to print out some more information for you to give to your doctor. Hold tight I'll be right back."

A silence came across the room. Everything got cold. Karl and I just looked at each other, then we looked down at this pamphlet about late term abortions with pictures of kids on it. *Some advertisement.* I thought to myself.

I didn't know what to say. Karl shook his head in disbelief. The doctor returned, and I blurted out, "What about the testing?"

She looked puzzled.

"I took tests early in my pregnancy and they screened for birth defects. Why didn't anyone tell me then that something was wrong?"

"Your numbers came back very close. If it was just 0.01% more you would have been flagged, but because you weren't the system didn't catch it nor did the doctors, but because you were so close to borderline birth defects, it normally means something is wrong," she said.

"Why weren't we notified? I don't understand." I said with tears in my eyes.

She just shook her head and said "I'm sorry, I know this was not the news you were expecting."

A baby that I hadn't been sure I even wanted to keep, a baby growing in my womb, a baby whom I grew to love, was now in trouble and there was nothing I could do.

After the doctor left the room, we grabbed our things and walked back towards the car. Once inside the car, we just sat there for a minute trying to process everything that just happened.

"Down Syndrome?" Karl said, as he reached for his phone.

We googled the definition of Down Syndrome seeing as how neither one of us knew anyone with it. When we googled it, it said that it was *A genetic condition in which a person has an extra chromosome. We started googling pictures of people with Down Syndrome. They all looked alike, they all had slanted eyes, large tongues, and small faces. Most of the pictures showed kids and they were all short. The thing that stood out most to me was a description saying that people with Down Syndrome had intellectual challenges, and some of them had a medical characteristic like a heart condition, or intestinal condition, some of them had a chance of getting cancer, some of them are hard of hearing,* and the list went on and on.

As I read them out loud Karl interrupted me and said, "Well our son already has two of those characteristics".

I just looked at him. "But everything is going to be okay," he said.

The ride back home was silent. My mind was racing thinking about what happened. I kept replaying the scene over and over in my head. I began to think about what the future would look like, and if there would be a future for him.

Karl grabbed my hand and held it saying, "Everything is going to be okay".

He was always the understanding, optimistic one, but I wasn't so sure. I thought about all the procedures the doctor said our baby would need right away. Would he be okay? Would I be okay? What is he going to look like? How will these procedures work? Every single question I had replayed in my mind. My anxiety and stress level went through the roof.

The next few days seemed like a blur. I had to carry on like normal. I mean, there was nothing I could do. We informed my family, and they were supportive but also in shock like we were. They asked me all these questions I didn't have answers for. I don't know if it was too much stress, but Friday morning, March 9, 2012, just 4 days after we left the specialist, I was getting ready for work, I started to feel something wet and warm flowing down my leg.

"Oh shoot" I said. I thought I was peeing on myself. I hurried and sat on the toilet just to see it was not urine, but blood, and it was everywhere! I didn't panic. I was quite calm. I immediately called my mother, then Karl who was already at work. My next call was to 911. I needed an ambulance quickly! I didn't even have a bag packed. I was only thirty-three and half weeks! I still had so much to do. I had so much running through my mind. Honestly, I think I just gave up.

I remember telling the paramedics to take me to the hospital where I saw the specialist, which was 30 minutes away.

"Are you sure?" They kept asking me as they saw the amount of blood I was losing.

"Yes!" I demanded. "I have to go back to that hospital. I just saw the doctor there and they told me I needed to go there if something went wrong."

They didn't give me any push back. We drove to the hospital. I remember laying on the stretcher in the back of the ambulance texting the people I knew, and contacting my job, as if this was normal.

I started having contractions, but I think I was in so much shock, I couldn't feel them. The paramedic who rode in the back with me kept saying "Let me know when you are having a contraction so I can time them."

I couldn't think straight enough to keep up with them. I felt them but didn't feel the pain. I remember them taking me out of the back of the ambulance, and I remember a team of six to eight nurses and doctor's waiting for me as I was wheeled in. The doctor who tended to me was a middle-aged white woman who also appeared pregnant. She was at the head of the bed and looked fearful as she asked me how I was feeling. In my head, I was still processing everything that was going on. I didn't have time to be in pain. I was worried about me having this baby so early.

They took me directly to the operating room and prepped me. Everyone was moving so fast. I laid there helplessly, trying to understand what was going on.

"She's losing a lot of blood," I could hear one nurse say. "Call the bank and tell them we need blood stat!" I heard another say.

They were asking me tons of questions and I was unsure I was answering correctly because I began to fade in and out of consciousness. I was fighting to stay awake because I wanted to know what was happening. I needed to know if Kayden was okay.

The doctor came over, "If we can't stop your bleeding, I am putting you to sleep and we are taking the baby. Do you give us permission?"

I nodded my head as the oxygen mask was placed on my face. Less than five minutes later, I was being put under. I felt like I couldn't breathe at all. I kept pulling the mask down. After some calming direction from the team, I was able to breathe. I began to count to ten. By the time I got to the number three, I was waking up in the recovery room.

My eyes fluttered. I could see my mom sitting at my feet in a chair. Karl hadn't made it from work yet. Everything happened so fast! I tried to sit up as the nurse walked over to me asking me how I was feeling? I wondered why everyone kept asking me that. I was in a hospital after giving birth to a premature and special needs son. How was I supposed to feel? But I was so groggy, I couldn't answer her.

Just then, I remembered something! I put my hands on my shrunken stomach, fearing the worst. "Where's my baby?!"

"He's in the Intensive Care Unit," the nurse said calmly. "He's just fine." I sat back in the bed relieved that we both made it.

"You lost a lot of blood" the nurse said to me as I looked at her taking my vitals.

"What happened?" I asked my mom who was looking confused.

"We had to give you several blood transfusions," said the nurse.

Not even sure what that entailed, I just put my hands back over my stomach. "Mom, have you seen Kayden?"

"Not yet" she said, shaking her head.

"I want to see my baby." I said to the nurse who was taking my blood pressure.

"We will get you moved into a room and then you will be able to see him," the nurse assured me.

It would be hours later before I was moved into a room, and I was still out of it. By the time Karl arrived by my side, I asked him if he'd seen Kayden and he said no. Another nurse came in to check my vitals and see if I wanted food.

"How are you feeling?" she asked me.

"I want to see my baby! Where is my baby?"

"Let me go check," she said and left the room.

Karl asked what happened, and I told him the story. I sat up in the bed, agitated that I still hadn't seen Kayden. I felt ignored. Before I knew it, the door flung open and two people dressed in what looked like space suits, entered the room pushing a foil-covered spaceship. My eyes got big and Karl stood up.

I asked, "Is that my baby?"

They pushed him closer to me. He was in a tiny incubator wrapped up so tight in blankets and foil-looking coverings on top. They cracked a little piece of the blanket so we could see a tiny little head and some hair. I felt a little relief but quickly noticed paperwork, and bags attached to the incubator. I turned to get out of the bed as if I did not just have major surgery.

"Where are you guys taking my baby?" I yelled. I was pissed. The nurse must have heard me because she came flying into the room. "Where are you all going with him?" They quickly covered him back up.

Something wasn't right. The woman in the spacesuit looked at the nurse, then she looked at me and said, "He is being transferred to a hospital in Oakland where they can better take care of him."

We were in Walnut Creek, a 40-minute drive away. They quickly rolled him back out the door and left. Tears immediately rolled down my face. I had yet to see or touch or hold Kayden and now they were taking him away from me? I lost it!

"Get me out of here! There's no way I am staying here, and you all are taking my baby to another hospital without me!"

The nurse tried to calm me down and be as polite as she could. "Go get the doctor" I demanded. "This is some bullshit. You guys can't just take my baby; I haven't even seen him!"

I was crying, cussing, and fussing all at the same time. The doctor finally came into the room, and I demanded to be sent to the same hospital Kayden was transferred to. Karl was trying to calm me down, but it didn't work. I wanted blood, and even more, I wanted my baby. The doctor said he could not guarantee I would be able to go there, but I refused to take no for an answer! I wasn't trying to hear about policies, procedures, or precautions. I told Karl to grab all my stuff, unplug me from the machines and get me out. Karl knew I was dead serious and begged the doctor to find out if I could be moved. Barely able to move, I began to unhook myself from the machines. I wasn't about to wait on anybody. I wasn't going to allow Kayden to be away from me. No one discussed anything with me. No one said he would be moved or asked my permission.

"Karl, let's go," I demanded. He was in shock that I'd removed all the cords and monitors from myself.

I didn't know what was going on. The nurse came running back into the room and said she had good news. The hospital had a room for me and was willing to take me there by ambulance as a safety measure since I just had a major procedure hours earlier. They couldn't risk me leaving the hospital against the doctor's orders, but they were able to make it work if I allowed the hospital to treat me, stopped being belligerent, and let them finish their jobs. I agreed because I knew I was that much closer to seeing my Kayden.

It was 11:00 pm when I arrived in Oakland. I was sick from all the medication and tired, but I was determined to see and hold my baby. I couldn't understand why everyone was so nonchalant about me not being able to see him. Karl had followed the ambulance to Oakland to make sure I was settled in, but he was so tired that I sent him home. The medicine finally started to wear off, and he had a long drive back home. I assured him it would be okay for him to go get some rest since my mother was watching our other son.

There are certain people in our lives who we'll never forget, and a nurse I had, is one. She was kind and gentle with me as she helped me get situated in my new hospital room. She told me what she was going to do, and how she was going to clean me, bring me my meds and give me something to eat. I began to cry. She stopped dead in her tracks and comforted me.

"Are you in pain?" Sheila asked. "What do you need?"

I looked at her, "I just want to see my baby!"

I wouldn't know if he was okay until I put eyes on him myself. It's what every mother needs in order to be okay. We don't care what we look like or how much trauma we experienced. The pain doesn't cease until we see our child.

She stood up and put her hands on her hips. "You haven't seen your baby yet?"

"No!" I said in tears. "I just want to see him. That is it!" Sheila assured me that she was going to personally take me to the NICU.

I felt so much relief to hear an answer, *FINALLY* I thought, someone heard me. *Why do I even have to continue to ask to see my child?* I kept thinking.

I did not fully understand what it meant when I was told "Your baby will have complications and need surgery." Nor was I clear about what happens when you have a baby prematurely. No one explained anything to me, and everything happened so fast. I didn't put two and two together, and I certainly didn't assume they would take my baby right away, make sure he's okay, put him in an incubator, put tubes in him, I didn't know any of that. Heck, I didn't even know what the NICU was. All I knew was that I needed to lay eyes on my baby.

It was after midnight and, by this time, the hospital was quiet. The nurse got me cleaned up, she helped me get dressed, slipped on my socks and house shoes, threw on my robe, she even brushed my hair back for me. She was an angel.

"Now, let's go see your baby" she said proudly as she wheeled me through the dark, empty hospital.

I was so happy I could not do anything but cry and before you know it, I was in front of the NICU doors waiting to see and hold my baby for the very first time since giving birth to him.

#IAMSTRONG

CHAPTER 6

What Does Not Kill You Makes You Stronger

THE NEXT FEW DAYS IN the hospital were very grey for me. It was a difficult time because I had just given birth to a baby prematurely. I knew they said he would need surgery on his heart and his intestines. I knew he was only 4lbs, and I even knew they said he had Down Syndrome, but when I looked at his little face and laid his little body on my chest, none of those things crossed my mind. Every morning I woke up in the hospital eager to see Kayden. It was a totally different birthing experience from having my first son. With my first son, I gave birth to him, he stayed in the room with me the entire four days we were in the hospital, then when it was time to go home. We packed our stuff and we went home to start our new life together as a family. This experience was so opposite, Kayden was going to remain in the hospital after I was discharged; I never processed that in my mind. It was hard enough that I had to go see my son in another part of the hospital.

There was a whole process I had to endure whenever I wanted to go see Kayden who is in the NICU. Before you could enter the NICU, you had to wash your hands and arms with this special soap for about 1 ½ minute. Then they give you clean gowns to put on which was not required but strongly recommended. I always took one. I did not want to take any risks around my baby. Once you did that, you were let inside a set of double doors where you would see tons of these tiny incubators with these tiny babies in them. They looked like tiny spaceships, with different medical devices connected to them. Kayden's incubator was towards the back of the NICU, and I had to walk past all the tiny, helpless babies and their families. It was sad because, even though I was going through the same thing, I felt bad for the other moms. We all have these sick babies in these rooms together, all helpless and depending on the nurses and staff to do what we could not. Some of the moms would be crying, some would be smiling and playing with their babies, some nursing their babies, but it was always eventful walking through the NICU halls, but you couldn't help but empathize with one another.

I would go visit Kayden from the time I woke up until it was time for me to go to sleep. There were two rules in the NICU. There was no sleeping or eating anywhere inside, so you had to leave to do both. The nurses would have to literally make me go eat or go rest because I never wanted to leave his side. The nurses were so friendly and kind towards me, I knew they meant well. I knew Kayden's nurses on both shifts, and I knew every detail of what was going on around him. I knew how much he had eaten; I knew the last time they changed his diaper; I could tell who worked with him on certain days by how the blankets were folded in his incubator, or by how he was laying down. I did not miss a beat. I had no choice but to trust these people who were working and taking care of him around the clock, but I was going to learn as much as I could about them, and I was going to be as pleasant as I could around them. After all, when I was not there, they were the ones taking care of him. As hard as it was to get adjusted to the NICU life, I did well under the circumstances. My baby was growing, he seemed happy and I was satisfied with his care, but nothing could prepare me for what I was about to experience next.

I guess I had been spending too much time focused on Kayden that I never took into consideration that I would have to leave him there. The day I was discharged, my mother, Karl, and his friend, Cedric, came to pick me up. Kayden's doctor and my nurse explained everything to me about how Kayden needed to stay in the NICU until he became stronger but that I could come to visit him daily. I heard what they were saying, but it didn't really hit me that I would be leaving the hospital without my baby until we went down to the cafeteria after I was discharged. We had grabbed everything from the hospital room and since the baby's things could not go into the NICU, we had some of his things also. We were heading out towards the car when my husband wanted to stop and get some food from the hospital café. I could not eat anything; I was filled with many different emotions.

I kept thinking, "Oh my God, I am leaving my baby in this hospital."

We were all were sitting at the table. They were waiting on their orders when suddenly, it hit me like a ton of bricks.

"Oh my God," I said. I put my hands over my face and I just started bawling right there in the middle of the café. I couldn't speak, I couldn't move, and I couldn't hear anything that was going on around me. I just felt so empty and so hurt that I had to leave my baby, my helpless 4-pound baby in this hospital, and it had just hit me. Karl and my mother tried to console me the best they could, but I lost it. I was crying and hyperventilating so hard that I could not breathe. I was burning up and having a full anxiety attack. I could not gain control. Cedric instructed the food workers to pack their food to go so that they could take me to the car. I would not wish that feeling on any mother as long as I live. There are no words to describe the feeling of coming to a hospital pregnant, delivering your child, and leaving empty-handed. It is one of the worst feelings in the world. I just wanted to be there with him, I felt horrible and helpless, I did not want to leave, I was completely devastated and there was nothing I could do.

The ride home was quiet, Karl and my mom kept looking at me, consoling me to make sure I was okay, but I was not. They rolled the window down to get some air, but it didn't stop the tears from flowing down my face. No matter how awful I felt, I still had to go home and be a mother to my 1 1/2year old, a wife to my husband, and start this new life I never thought I would have. After my mother made sure I got in the house safely, she hugged me and went over to talk to Karl. She was concerned about me, and she was telling him to call her if he needed her. I'm sure it was hard for them to see me in distress and know there was nothing they could do about it. I just sat there staring at the wall trying to catch my breath. I felt like I was in a bad dream, and I was trying to wake up, but reality quickly set back in. Khalil came running into my arms. I hadn't seen him in almost a week! I hugged him, and I just cried even more. Karl came and took Khalil to the back and put him to bed after our short reunion. Karl got the bed ready for me to lay down but before I did that, I wanted to take a shower. I slowly walked to the bathroom, got in the shower, and continued to cry. As I was crying in the shower, I experienced something that I had never experienced before. In the midst of me bawling my eyes out, I felt this sudden peace. It was almost like I stopped crying immediately, and for a split second, I felt nothing. The shower had suddenly gotten bright, and, at first, I thought I was going to pass out; I thought I had been crying too much but then I looked up and I felt the presence of God come over me. It was like He was telling me that everything was going to be okay and, now more than ever, he needed me to be strong for Kayden. He reminded me that I could bear the burden, and my family depended on me. He told me, if I believed in him, and as long as I came to him, that he would supply all my needs and that he would bring baby Kayden home.

"Everything is going to be alright," I said. "God is with us." Just then I saw the name Emmanuel, the middle name Karl chose for Kayden when I was five months pregnant. This was a part of the plan. I thought, "Wow!"

I looked up again and the light was gone. I said out loud "Emmanuel." I proceeded to bathe and ran my face under the shower. I turned the shower off and stepped out of the tub. By the time I dried off I had realized that I had stopped crying. I went into Khalil's room to check on him; he was knocked out. I walked into my room where Karl had brought me some water, my medicine, and some roses. I smiled, walked over to him, and gave him a hug and after that, I laid down and went to sleep.

The next morning, I woke up feeling amazing. I felt as if I had a really good dream as if I was very well rested. I had a feeling, not of worry or of sadness, but that everything was going to be okay. I knew God was with me, and even more so, that he would be with Kayden. From that day on, I knew no matter what, we were going to be okay.

Over the next two and a half months my life flashed before my eyes. I did the same thing every day like clockwork. I would get up in the morning, pump my liquid gold (breast milk) for Kayden, drop Khalil off at daycare and go straight to the NICU. That 40-minute drive across the bay from Antioch to Oakland got easier day by day. Every day was a challenge because I still had to leave my baby there, but I had hope and I knew one day I would be driving home with him in the back seat so my trips to the hospital had gotten easier. I had to fix my mind on the future and what we were going to do once Kayden came home so I was not as worried about what was happening to him while he was there. I was there every step of the way and I felt happy knowing God was with me. Some days I would rock Kayden in the rocking chair and just read the Bible to him, sing songs to him, and other days I would leave him in the incubator and ask the doctors and nurses a series of questions. Every day I walked through those doors, I would take my notebook with me to write down things I saw or questions I had because I wanted to make sure I was on top of it and I didn't want to forget anything. Some days were harder than others, but I never allowed it to take me back to that place of helplessness and despair. Knowing I would get to see and hold my son who was fighting for his life was good enough for me. When it was time for Kayden to begin his surgeries, it was incredibly stressful. My family would always come to the hospital to support me, but at the end of the day, I had to be strong for them. Turns out they needed me more than I needed them. They needed me to assure them of what I already knew, which was that Kayden was going to be okay.

Or so I thought.

I recall an incident one night after Kayden's first corrective surgery to his intestines when he was diagnosed with something called Hirschsprung's disease. Hirschsprung's disease is when a part of the small intestines is not working properly, and it causes bloating, an enlarged stomach, and constipation. To correct it, the "dead" part had to be removed. The surgeon explained, in detail, the process of how that worked and what that looked like but the only thing I remember him saying is "We won't know how much of his intestines we will have to remove until we start the procedure."

That also meant that, if they had to remove all his intestines, he would have to have a colostomy bag. That is a bag connected to a hole on the outside of your stomach where the poop would go because without intestines, it would have no other place to go. I remember praying and asking God to please let that not be the case for Kayden. I paced the hospital waiting room the entire time they worked on him. I was so nervous and afraid, but I trusted God and I knew that he would do what is best.

After the surgery was over, I was right there when the team rolled Kayden back into the NICU. There were seven or eight nurses and surgeons and the doctor around him. The surgeon explained his surgery went well and that he did not need a colostomy and I was thrilled. I took a deep breath and sat down in the rocking chair inside the NICU and watched the team stand over him but then something hit my gut hard. I felt an instant sickness and I could tell something was not right. I did not panic, I held on to what God told me, and so I just sat back in that rocking chair and started to pray. Suddenly, all the machines Kayden was hooked up to started alarming and the sirens were going off for some reason. I didn't panic or move, but I knew God was sitting with me. I sat there in that rocking chair praying.

Kayden had coded and his heart rate drastically decreased. His breathing was slowing down at an alarming rate and the team went into panic mode. I watched as they scrambled around him trying to figure out what was wrong. I watched patiently while in prayer as they had to perform CPR and eventually use the machine to shock my baby's heart to wake him up. Then suddenly, the doctor told one of the nurses to get the adverse reaction medicine for the morphine they had given Kayden right after surgery for pain. I just watched helplessly, and I remember repeating, "God help my baby".

They quickly administered medicine to him through his IV in his little chest and within seconds, I could see his heart rate going back up on the monitors. The alarms started to quietly beep like normal and the team all took a deep breath of relief. The doctors checked Kayden and watched him for several moments before coming over to me.

"It turns out that Kayden cannot have morphine," the doctor said. "It immediately affects his heart, and he is far too weak for that type of pain medication but he's going to be alright. We will give him something else for pain, but we caught it, and he is going to make it."

"Oh, I know," I said with assurance. "God is with us and he knows!"

The doctor looked at me. I don't know how many mothers would have been as calm as I was, or if any of them have ever watched their child basically take their last breath in front of them but what I can tell you is that prayer is the ONLY thing that got me through. I do not know how I was able to do it, but GOD! From that day on, Kayden's medical records state he is "Allergic" to morphine, and he hasn't had it ever since.

After a few other procedures, some preparational classes, and trainings, after many prayers, tears, worries, and positive thoughts On May 25, 2012, I brought my baby home!

Kayden was so tiny, but he was so adorable. We were beyond ecstatic to finally be free from the NICU. His nurse even cried when he was being discharged and that made me feel so special because I knew she had taken very good care of him. As happy as I was that my baby was finally home, I was even more fearful now because of all the medication my son had to take. Not only that, but he was also still not able to drink milk, so I had to learn how to use a feeding pump and an NG tube, a feeding tube that is placed through the nostril and into the stomach for feedings. Kayden was also waiting to have his major heart surgery that summer because he was much too frail and small when he was released, and the doctors feared he wouldn't survive had they performed the surgery then.

We were finally all together at home where we belonged. Getting adjusted to a family of 4 with a one year old and a 2 ½-month-old baby boy was difficult, but nonetheless, we felt very blessed. Luckily for us, we were able to have some help from family and friends and we needed it. Kayden being at home was much different than the hospital because, in the NICU, the nurses did everything for me. Kayden was on twelve different medications when he came home, and I had twelve different alarms going off two to three times per day as reminders. We had even moved in our friend's daughter who was our boys' Godsister and Khalil's babysitter. She was always around us, anyway, watching and helping with Khalil or just visiting so it made sense to move her in to help us full time. With Karl working full time and me taking care of Kayden around the clock and still having to chase my toddler around, we needed all hands on deck. We had a routine and things started to look up for us until one day, I received an e-mail from my job stating that they were closing our office.

#IAMGRATEFUL

CHAPTER 7

Movin' On Up

I HAD NO IDEA HOW I was going to go back to work full time again and take care of this baby who needed around-the-clock care, but at least I was still being paid while we figured that all out. Karl worked full-time but he didn't make enough to support all of us and our bills. He was paying child support to Felicia every month, and we really could not afford to lose any money coming into our home. We made too much money for public assistance, but we were too poor to survive on just one income. I kept thinking about what my mother said when I told her I was pregnant with Kayden: "It's going to be harder, you can barely afford one!"

Then one day, Karl had come home from work not looking or feeling well at all. He had been complaining of headaches and chest pains for some time, but he would suppress his feelings because, like most parents, he was more concerned about the children, and he was also concerned about me. Karl had to retire from his semi-pro football career to take care of us, but he was still in good shape. After being convinced to go see the doctor, Karl was diagnosed with heart failure and his doctor recommended that he start taking medications immediately. The cardiologist prescribed three different medications for Karl to take daily, which he began right away but quickly realized how costly the medication was and how bad the medication made him feel so he slowly stopped taking them. I encouraged him to continue his medication and maybe even get it modified from his doctor, but he didn't listen.

Karl was always the levelheaded one in the relationship. Where I would stress and worry, he would always seem so relaxed. He knew he was the man of the house and after some struggles with my wanting to be strong and lead our family, I had to allow him to be the man. He took pride in making sure we had everything we needed. He would go without to make sure we had what we needed which was a bad thing in this case because what he needed the most was that medication. I would stay on Karl about taking his medication and told him not to worry about the cost because we needed him alive, but Karl felt like he was fine. He completely stopped taking the medicine. I was already stressed and had my hands full with the boys. I didn't have the energy to keep fighting with him about it.

Between administering medications to my son daily, chasing my toddler, fighting with my husband to take better care of himself, and being fearful of what was going to happen to us since I'd been laid off, we were in a hole. We were behind on our rent, bills piled up, but thank God our landlords were Christians and in a position to help us. They knew what we'd been through, and we'd never fallen behind, and they were beyond understanding. One day the landlord called us and said God had spoken to him and his wife concerning me and my family. They were willing to lower the rent and accept whatever we could give in agreement to allow us to continue living there while we sorted our life out. We were so grateful and in awe of the constant reminder that God was really with us. It was embarrassing and very hard for us to be in such a vulnerable position, but we needed the help. The stress levels in our home were high. Karl and I were constantly at each other's throats. The kids were driving us crazy; I knew I needed to work but I couldn't work because of the demands and needs of the kids and Karl's health had really started taking a toll on him. We knew we needed a new start, but we weren't sure how to go about it. We loved California, and all our family was there, but the cost of living had risen above our means. Something needed to change.

Karl and I had discussed moving away from California but never entertained it until the day Karl suggested we move to Atlanta. The funny thing is, when Karl and I first started dating, I'd shared with him that in five years I wanted to move to Atlanta. I'd lived there for a year right after college and I fell in love with the city. It was very different from California. They had real trees, fresh air, everyone was nice, and there was something for people of all ages to do. I'd seen a lot of successful Black people own homes and start businesses in Atlanta, and more importantly, the cost of living was way cheaper. Karl never wanted to leave his daughter, who was living with Felicia in San Francisco at that time, but he'd gotten so frustrated with not being able to see her, he'd given up. Felicia wanted to hurt Karl so bad, she'd stopped allowing his daughter to come visit us. Karl felt like since Felicia wouldn't allow their daughter to see him anyway, we may as well move so he could better himself for his daughter, his boys, and myself. He always held on to hope that one day his daughter would be able to come to Georgia to see him. So, when Karl said to me "Let's just move to Georgia," I knew he had been pushed over the edge.

This would mean a new start, a new chance for us. God was certainly with us because I had reached out to my uncle, who was relocating from Atlanta to Texas, to ask him what he was doing with his house. Coincidentally, he stated he was going to call me because he heard we were moving to Atlanta in hopes to rent his house out to us. Timing is everything! We had a place to stay. So far, all signs were pointing to move. We were excited about moving, but my family was in disbelief. They didn't understand why we wanted to move so far away because we needed help. But I knew God's hand was on us and things would get better. This is a journey we had to take. I called my best friend Neicy and she was excited for us. She thought it would be a great idea and an opportunity for a new start. Neicy and I had met in high school when we were 14 years old. She knew me like the back of her hand. We shared a lot of experiences together including a lot of first moments. We were inseparable until we both went off to college. She attended an HBCU in Florida while I attended my HBCU in Tennessee. We remained close and visited each other as often as possible. I valued her opinion because I did not have a lot of friends. Neicy would always be honest with me whether I wanted to hear it or not. If she thought us moving to Atlanta was a good idea I was sold! Truthfully, I was already sold but that would just put the icing on the cake for me.

I explained to Neicy that I was crazy enough to believe God was moving us for a reason and in the midst of one of the hardest times in our lives, the best thing for us to do was start over. I trusted God and my husband was in full support of it. My mother ended up giving us a huge fundraiser/going away party in honor of our son Kayden and our move. All our friends and our family showed up and showed out. They showered us with more gifts and money than we could have ever imagined. The money from the fundraiser, coupled with the savings we had and the layoff money I received from my job, we had close to seventeen thousand dollars! As nervous as we were to be away from our families and everything we knew, there was no turning back now. We knew this was nothing but God because He was making a way out of no way for us. We purchased our plane tickets, got rid of everything we could not sell, and shipped our car. We were on our way to start our new life in Marietta, Georgia. Things were starting to look back up again.

#IAMCONFIDENT

CHAPTER 8

Live and Learn

MY UNCLE HAD A SMALL-TOWN house in East Cobb Marietta, Georgia. It sat in the hills in a private neighborhood that had a pond, a trail, and a lot of stuck-up nosey neighbors but it was our new home. The backyard was beautiful and there were so many trees. The air smelled very different in the south, it smelled like nature, and I was thrilled. The townhouse was two stories, it had three bedrooms and two and a half bathrooms, perfect for us. Our kid's Godsister, Angel, moved to Georgia with us in hopes to start her life over as well. We all needed a change of scenery. We paid my uncle rent a year in advance so we wouldn't have to worry while Karl looked for a job. Georgia was beautiful, we finally settled in and tried to get our life back.

I quickly found all the resources I needed for Kayden, who was now two years old. He was growing up and being a busy body just like his brother. They always kept me on my toes. Kayden still required a lot of different vitamins and medicine, not to mention he was receiving physical, occupational, and speech therapy. One thing that shocked me the most about Georgia was the number of Black therapists and doctors available to us. Being from California your doctor was either White, Indian, or Asian so it was exciting to see people who looked like me have such rewarding careers. I was so shell-shocked that I made sure that all of Kayden's doctors and therapists were black. I had never seen a black person in the medical field before. Kayden had a pediatrician, a cardiologist, a gastroenterologist, three therapists, and a nutritionist all on his team, and I was responsible for making sure his medical team was intact. In the beginning, it was difficult keeping up with all of Kayden's needs, but I quickly learned how to be organized and detailed. I often prayed for patience and strength. Not only was I a mother, but I was also a mother to a child with special needs, and my job was to make sure he was safe and to live the best quality of life I could give him. As a matter of fact, before we left California, with the help of my mother, we filed a lawsuit against the hospital for misdiagnosing and not catching Kayden's diagnosis in a timely manner. If I couldn't give him everything he needed and wanted, I was sure the hospital should.

After a week, Karl was offered a position working at a furniture factory close to our neighborhood. Khalil was turning four that summer, and I was working on enrolling him into school. I was very happy because having two children less than two years apart while dealing with the health issues of Karl and Kayden was a lot. I often felt like a zombie always on the go. Someone always needed my attention, to be fed, to be changed, not to mention Kayden was still on a feeding tube. He would still need another surgery for it to be removed. Shortly after that procedure, we found out Kayden was having hearing problems and another surgery was suggested to correct it. I knew moving to Georgia wouldn't fix all my problems, but I was still excited to see what it had to offer. Our lives didn't slow down; it just shifted a little.

Sometimes you could be so caught up in life events, children, changes, and forget you are still a spouse, and your mate needs you just as much. My mind was always fixated on the boys and making sure they had what they needed. Karl's mind was fixated on providing, but we couldn't seem to get on the same page. We were settling into our new lives living in this new state and we were always on the go. I wasn't paying attention to my marriage, and Karl had begun to feel like our relationship didn't matter to me anymore and we bumped heads. I felt my other responsibilities were a priority. At the end of my long days, I was tired!

I slept when I could, and if we had free time, we were taking our boys out to the park, or to play, or I was cleaning and doing housework. There was always something that needed to be done, but Karl and I rarely had any alone time, and our troubles began. My attention was needed everywhere, and I was only one person. I didn't have a chance to sit down and talk to Karl about our relationship because he suddenly began to have black-out episodes.

Karl's blood pressure would be so high his vision would become impaired. Once, I rushed him to the hospital when he'd blacked out one evening. He had a habit of not letting me know when he wasn't feeling well and waited all day to tell me he was experiencing shortness of breath and chest pains. It aggravated me because he knew if he'd told me, I would've taken him to the ER. When we arrived at the ER, nurses took his blood pressure; they were in shock. They checked four times before accepting 225/200.

The nurses kept asking him, "How are you still alive right now?"

They were all in disbelief. I knew he had heart failure and was supposed to be taking his medication. I had no idea his blood pressure was so high. I already had a child who needed my attention 24/7 I did not have the energy to force a grown man to do anything he did not want to do. It's like the old saying "You can lead a horse to water but you can't make him drink it." The hospital was able to lower his blood pressure. He finally started to take the medication regularly, but the damage was already done.

A week later, we went to see the cardiologist. Karl was afraid because of his previous health battles, and I was more focused on how I could juggle everything. I went through cycles of guilt for not doing enough, and anger at Karl for not doing enough. It was hard not knowing what was going to happen. I stressed myself out so much worrying about the future I often made myself sick.

After a series of tests, scans, and vital checks, the cardiologist said Karl would have to continue taking blood pressure medications daily in an attempt to slow down his heart failure. The surprising news was Karl was referred to an endocrinologist. He was in kidney failure due to his high blood pressure and needed to be placed on the donor list. We stared at each other, baffled.

"What does that mean?" Karl asked the doctor.

"Your kidneys are not functioning at the level they are supposed to be. Which is causing the aches, pains, and spells you're having. That, coupled with heart failure, and you not taking medication has taken a toll on your body."

I thought back to when we lived in California and how Karl was told to start his medication. I selfishly thought about what this meant for me. How could this happen? I'd told him to follow the doctor's instructions. Karl was obviously afraid, so I remained silent. The doctor instructed Karl to get dressed and let him know the endocrinologist would give him further information on his condition.

The next several months were tough for us. I felt bad for Karl but couldn't help my frustration. I'd be lying if I said I never thought how preventable the situation was. How was I going to do this? We were already in and out of the hospital with Kayden, and now Karl; I was trying to figure it all out. Angel had moved out to start on her own, and we had no other family. This was all on us, and truthfully, I felt it was all on me. I was working part-time to help with the bills. Karl was still working part-time. I was a full-time caregiver, wife, and mother, the boys were in school.

Then just when we thought things couldn't get any worse, we were hit with more news.

Our eldest son was diagnosed with ADHD.

My son's teachers often told us Khalil would be impulsive in class and would react without thinking. His behavior was so random, he was often in the principal's office. The teachers said Khalil was very smart and knew the material but couldn't be still. Every time he got in trouble at school, he would get punished at home. I didn't understand why he was misbehaving, and I thought it was because his brother was getting more attention and he felt left out. Everyone knows negative attention is better than no attention for a child. Khalil was acting out and I blamed myself. I thought Khalil needed me to be a better mom to him.

Khalil's teacher suggested having him evaluated by a psychologist. I didn't need to add anything else to my plate, but I had to figure out what was going on with him. I was stressed to the max with everything going, but I couldn't ignore the needs of my son. I didn't have time to be in denial, so I trusted his teacher and took him to a child psychologist. The doctor gave Khalil a series of tests and evaluations. A week later the official diagnosis of ADHD was received. He was too young for medications, but we were given a book of strategies to try. The diagnosis was a relief because it helped us understand Khalil's behavior, but I had yet another diagnosis in my home to deal with. A child with Down Syndrome and Autism, a husband with heart failure and kidney failure, and now my eldest son was diagnosed with ADHD, the weight of my cape increased.

I could no longer hold it together. I did not know where to go or who to turn to. I just had to cry and break down in silence. I shut down, became numb to everything and everyone. I had friends but felt none of them could help me or understand how I was feeling. I had family, but they could only extend money and that would only go so far. I had my husband, but he was going through so much with his health. Besides, I was secretly harboring ill feelings towards him. I resented him for not taking care of himself. I felt alone. I wasn't talking to Karl, my friends, or my family. I was at the lowest point in my life. Everyone demanded my attention. I couldn't eat, wasn't sleeping, and felt like a zombie. I beat myself up for feeling vulnerable and helpless. I was the strong one. I was drained mentally and physically, and to make matters harsher, I found out Karl was seeking attention from another woman.

#IMATTER

CHAPTER 9

Love Don't Live Here Anymore

SOMETIMES, MEN CANNOT COMMUNICATE WHAT they need, feel, or want, and they simply shut down or seek elsewhere to get what they feel they are lacking. For Karl, it was communication, affection, and attention. He wanted me to pay more attention to him. He wanted us to cuddle more and go out. I wasn't trying to hear any of that because we had too many other things to deal with. I felt he was demanding more attention than I could give, and he was being selfish for not understanding my point of view or how my responsibilities impacted me. I was tired, stressed, and secretly fighting depression. Karl was focused on his needs and what he wanted. Meanwhile, I was worried about his health, my mental health, and our children.

I made his appointments and ensured he stayed on top of them. I did the grocery shopping, drove back and forth to the hospitals, therapies, and schools. I did it all, we were still struggling financially, emotionally and our relationship became strained. Neither of us felt seen or heard about how all the pressures were making us feel. We were both stubborn. The less we expressed our feelings, the less we communicated, the further we started to drift apart. We loved each other but didn't know how to balance each other's needs and wants, nor did we communicate about them.

There was constant tension in our home. Karl always had an attitude, and I always ignored him, which upset him more. Either we were going to figure out a resolution or things were going to remain the same. It seemed like he only wanted was sex and affection and didn't care about me, and as his wife, I was supposed to have sex with him whenever he desired. Sex was not a priority to me. Besides if he was tired and not feeling well all the time due to his health, how did he always have energy for sex? It didn't make sense to me and the more he asked, the angrier I became. When it got to the point, I began to zone out during sex, I decided that until we fixed our issues, I didn't want him touching me. I was not turned on, didn't feel sexy, and wasn't in the mood at all. No contact wasn't going to work for Karl.

On a rare occasion when the boys were napping, Karl was asleep, and I was cleaning the house and trying to organize while it was quiet, and something hit the pit of my stomach to check the cell phone records. Me being the inspector gadget that I was, went straight to it. I didn't have a reason to think anything was going on. I was consumed the way my life was, that maybe I didn't catch the signs, but I always listen to myself. I went straight to our cell phone account records to look at his call and text logs. I noticed a number he called and often received calls from. Some of their conversations lasted upwards to 30 minutes, something wasn't right. Karl had one friend in Georgia and I knew his number. Everyone else was family and friends from California and doctors or pharmacies. I instantly felt a huge blow to my chest before I even confirmed anything, but I knew it was something.

I immediately dialed the number. It didn't matter if I seemed crazy or insecure, I was going to find out what was going on.

"Hello?" A woman answered the phone in a deep sultry voice.

I had to react quickly before she hung up because of the awkward silent pause. "Who is this?" I asked as if she called my phone.

Her tone changed immediately. "This is Tracey. Who is this?

"This is the wife of the man you have been talking to," I said as I proceeded to go on. "I don't know how you know my husband, Karl, but it appears he's been talking to you lately and I'm trying to get some clarity on your relationship with him."

"Wife?" She said in shock. "I didn't know he was married!"

"Well, I am sorry that he lied to you, but he is married five years and has three children," I said.

"How did you meet him?" I asked her.

"We met online a few weeks ago," she said. "But he never told me he was married."

"Are you guys having sex?"

"You're going to have to talk to him about that," she said with an attitude.

At this point, nothing else she said mattered because I was reading all the text messages between them confirming who she was. I already knew the answer. I just wanted to hear what she had to say.

"Well, of course, I am going to talk to him," I said. "Don't call or text his phone now that you know the truth".

She didn't say anything. I simply hung up the phone. She'd been texting his phone, unbeknownst to her, I had his phone in my hand the entire time. She was pissed and was asking him why I was calling her phone and why did he lie to her. I guess in her mind she saw a future with him and really thought she found a good guy. He posed as a single father who recently moved to Georgia to start over. I saw a collage she made with pictures he'd sent her, and she added a few of herself and it read "together forever" and "I love you". He never responded. The fact that he lied to her let me know he didn't really care for this woman, but he lied to me, and worse, he betrayed me.

I stood in the kitchen with his phone in my left hand and my phone in the right. My blood was boiling! I was angry! Not to mention hurt, embarrassed, and sad. This woman was still calling his phone! I turned it off. I wasn't mad at her. She didn't know about me. Nevertheless, every negative thought went through my mind. How could he do this to me? Why would he hurt me? How dare he do this to me with all we were going through? He wasn't even in the right tax bracket to cheat!

I thought about our children, divorce, and prepared to be a single mother in a state with no family. Out of pure anger and impulsiveness, I ran up the stairs, busted open our bedroom door, aimed for his head, and threw his phone! Still half asleep, he sat up, grabbed his head, but before he could get a word out, I asked him who Tracey was.

"How could you do this to our family?" I questioned and accused him all in the same breath because I already knew the truth. He remained silent. He buried his head in the palm of his hands and shook his head. I'd told him years ago any choices he made would impact all of us. I gave him thirty-day notice to get the hell out. I was done. I marched right back downstairs, grabbed my keys, and drove away.

If I didn't leave that house, I was going to hurt him, and I didn't want my children to see that. I wanted to run him over and keep going, but I had too much to lose. During my ride around Atlanta, I reread the messages over and over in my mind. Visions of them being together came into my psyche. When did he have time to cheat? He was always home! Nothing made sense. How would it be for our boys without Karl living there? All Kayden and Khalil knew were us all being together. They loved their father, and he was a really good dad to them, but I couldn't see myself staying in a relationship where I was unhappy. I wasn't the type of woman to stay in an unhappy relationship for the sake of the children. That would only lead to resentment towards him. While I didn't marry to get a divorce, getting married to be hurt wasn't on my list either. I was so messed up in the head I couldn't think straight. I had a migraine. There was no excuse for his behavior, and we could've talked about this if he'd just given me more time. Nothing warranted this kind of hurt.

My eyes were swollen from crying and my head ached, but I had to get myself together because my kids, nor Karl would see my hurt when I returned home. Our boys had never heard us yell or argue before because we rarely did. If we had a disagreement, we never discussed it in front of them. I took deep breaths and I tried to think of anything else to help stop the tears. My strength had to show for the boys and myself. I gripped my cape and thought I had never seen my mother cry. It didn't mean she didn't hurt. It meant to me that she was strong. I was striving to be just like her at that moment. Growing up, my mother was tough and had high expectations of me. She was a fighter who didn't take mess from anyone. She rarely showed emotions.

It's disturbing now that I think about it. I knew she was my mom, and she was there, but I often wondered if she cared because she never showed her emotions. Whenever I did show emotions, it made me feel weak and stupid. Even though I had every right to be emotional at that time. I didn't get a lot of affection from my mom. All that learned behavior did was make me suppress my feelings. If I cried, I better do it fast, wipe my tears and move on. During a time when I was the most vulnerable, I still thought about being strong. Being raised with tough love and a unaffectionate mother will do that to you.

I pulled into my cul-de-sac, took a deep breath, and wiped my face. The quick escape was over, and reality had set back in. This wasn't a dream. This was happening, and I still have to move on with my day and my life. The thing about marriage is there is no such thing as running away or simply being done. I had to face the inevitable. I was still a mother with responsibilities and duties. My kids didn't deserve to have half of me or see me upset or crying. I had to put on my big girl panties and handle my business.

I walked through the door to see the boys eating in front of the TV. How could he do this to my kids? I got mad all over again. Every time I looked at my boy's faces, I felt the pain caused by the actions of their father. I felt bad for them. I headed upstairs to face this new demon, which was my husband. I walked upstairs, opened my bedroom door, and to my surprise, Karl was sitting in a chair next to the window. His head was hung down, and he was fully dressed. He'd put his clothes in garbage bags and stacked them next to him.

"Going somewhere?" I asked him.

His phone was still on the bed powered off. I didn't know what he was doing. I wanted to stomp his head in but maintained my composure. He looked at me. Part of me didn't care, but I knew he didn't have money to go. He didn't have his own car because we shared one.

"Well, you said you don't want to be with me anymore, and I was going to have to leave," he said. "So, I just packed my stuff".

"Where are you going?" I asked.

"I don't know." He said, "but I know you don't want me around and I understand."

I could tell he knew he'd messed up and the look of disappointment and hurt was all over his face. I cared, but I didn't. I was angry and upset, but I knew this fool couldn't go anywhere.

"I said I would give you 30 days to get your stuff together," I told him. "You don't have any money, no car, and are thousands of miles away from home. You have nothing and no help out here."

I was angry but understanding. "Just work, save your money, figure out if you want to go back to California or if you can go get an apartment somewhere here, but I want nothing from you," I said angrily.

"I'm not going back to California." Karl said.

"Okay, that's on you. Whatever you need to do to get yourself together, do it!" I walked out of the room.

The next couple of weeks were trying. No matter how much I was hurting, I still had to wake up and get out of bed every day. I still worked, took care of our boys, and still cared for Karl too. I was in a dark place but had to smile when I wanted to cry and be okay knowing I wasn't. I was not ready to deal with my reality. When your spouse breaks the marriage vows, it breaks your heart. Our first reaction is to react, but truthfully, you should never make quick decisions out of anger, desperation, or fear of the unknown. The most devastating part of being cheated on was dealing with the love that remained. Love doesn't just go away, but neither does the distrust. I didn't stop to process anything, I kept moving and stayed busy. I was avoiding the obvious. But whenever I thought about it, I was hurt all over again. I was tired of feeling that way. Something had to change, and decisions had to be made.

Karl and I were barely talking. I had nothing. I didn't even look him in his face. Whenever he asked to talk, I declined and told him I wasn't ready. My repeated refusals to converse upset him, and he eventually offered to leave until I was ready.

"Absolutely not!" I told him, which puzzled him. He didn't get to leave because my pain made him feel bad.

"You hurt me!" I told him. "So, you are going to sit here and deal with it," I said angrily. "You are going to sit here and take me being angry, ignoring you, not touching you, and just wait until I am ready to talk, you don't deserve sympathy from me!"

He just looked at me and let me talk. It was the most talking I'd done in weeks. I'd been going about my normal routine while ignoring him, and it was killing him. He never knew if I was going to snap or simply leave. He wanted forgiveness and to apologize but wouldn't give him the chance for either. For a month, I didn't say one word to him. The hardest part was no one knew. I hadn't told anyone about what was happening. I didn't want to hear anything negative or positive either. I was numb and stayed away from family and friends.

I spent that time talking to God praying for a miracle. I begged Him to help me decide. I wanted to move forward but wasn't sure how. Would I stay married or not? Would I trust him again if I stayed? Would I feel stupid? Did I feel stuck because we have children? Was I strong enough to care for them alone? The thing that really made me mad was questions about Karl's needs. Where would he go? How would he survive? What if something happened to him? The truth is, I beat myself up and felt stupid because beneath all my anger and hurt, I still loved Karl! I loved him and was mad about it. Why did I care about him? He'd hurt me, probably would do it again. I was all over the place and didn't want to forgive him. Regardless, if I stayed with him or not, I knew I had to forgive him. I knew forgiving him was for me. I wanted my peace, my freedom, my mind and spirit back; forgiving him is how I would get it.

One Saturday morning the kids were playing downstairs, and Karl was in the bathroom. I walked in, closed the door, and sat on the edge of the tub. He washed his hands, grabbed a towel to dry them, and stood against the door. I didn't know what I wanted to say, but I knew I had to say something. The pain was eating me up inside and I could no longer be quiet. I talked and talked and talked. He stood, in silence, and let me get everything out. It was as if I was having a conversation with myself weighing the good and bad, trying to decide what I wanted to do.

I reminded him of all the time, energy, love, and sacrifices I had put into our marriage, which made him a better man, father, husband, and lover. I upgraded him, and none of that was supposed to be in vain, and it would be foolish to lose it over a 20-minute sexual encounter. I was clear that I was with him because I loved him and wanted him, not because I needed him.

"You're a great father to your kids, a gentleman, you cook, clean, hand me your checks on payday, massage my feet, and worship the ground I walk on, but I will give all of that up in order to be happy."

With tears in his eyes, "I know I messed up and I am sorry. I don't want to lose my family; I love you and my kids. I don't know why I did that; I just need help. I need to be able to talk to you. I'll do whatever I need to not lose you."

I looked at him, unmoved. I needed to let him know how serious this was for me. "What you are not going to do is keep breaking my heart. If I do take you back, this is it! There are no more other chances" I said angrily.

I felt myself leaning towards forgiveness, and anger crept in. The unknown scared me.

"Can I just have a hug?" He asked me.

Before I could answer, he walked over and put his arms around me, and whispered. "I don't want to lose you. You are the best thing that ever happened to me."

I just sat there. I didn't want a hug or apology. I had no clue what I wanted. I just knew I was tired of feeling untethered and something had to give.

#IAMMORETHANENOUGH

CHAPTER 10

Forgive or not to forgive?

A WEEK LATER, I WAS still undecided about my marriage and received the most devastating news ever. My grandmother had passed away.

"God, what else?" I cried out.

My grandmother and I were extremely close. So close that I was born on her birthday. I loved making her laugh, and even though she lived in California, we talked on the phone every day. My mother bought her a new smartphone so we could facetime each other. My grandmother was my rock. She instilled everything in me about grace, love, kindness, and forgiveness. I guess that's why her name was Grace because she possessed it and carried it well. My grandmother introduced me to Christ and taught me about unconditional love. She always told me how proud she was of me and all my accomplishments and was there for every important moment of my life from graduations to childbirth, she was there never missing a beat. When my family was against Karl and me being together early on in our relationship, she was the one who told me to follow my heart. She always loved Karl and was rooting for us. She believed in us. I just couldn't believe she was gone.

After I got the call, I packed the boys and myself and hopped on the next flight to California. I was mourning the loss of someone who meant the world to me and didn't care about the unfinished business of my marriage. I didn't call him to check on him and when he called to see how the boys were, I was mute. I couldn't deal with it. It was too much with the passing of my grandmother. I really didn't want to think about any of it.

Before I knew it, two weeks had gone by. We had a beautiful homegoing celebration for my grandmother. My family and I were packing things away at her house, sorting out her mail, and trying to grasp the reality that the matriarch of our family was gone. I stumbled across a wooden cross in her nightstand. It was the size of the palm of my hand and had Mark 11:25 engraved on it. "And when you stand praying, if you hold anything against anyone, forgive them, so that your father in heaven may forgive you, your sins." I read the scripture over and over and sat there twenty minutes thinking about Karl. I kept hearing my grandmother say, "Forgiveness is forever." She was big on moving forward. She'd been through a lot in her life and always told me that forgiving myself and forgiving others was one of the keys to God's heart.

I said, "God, I don't want to be hurt again, but I don't want to break up my family, and I refuse to be in a place of unhappiness. But if You would just tell me what to do, give me a sign, I will obey."

Just then my phone rang, it was Karl.

"Hello?" I answered.

"Hey. How are you?" He asked.

"I'm here," I said, holding the cross in my hand.

"Listen," he said firmly. "I have been sitting in this house for weeks by myself and had a lot of time to think and talk to God. I can't afford to lose my family. I don't like this feeling of being alone, and quiet. I really want my family back. I miss my boys, and I need you and I am so sorry for hurting you. We can get counseling, whatever we need to do. I just can't do this without you." He said not taking a breath.

I looked down at the cross and looked up. "Really God?" I chuckled. I asked for a sign and I asked for guidance and He gave it to me. The truth is, I truly loved my husband. We'd come so far, and I didn't want to let go for one mistake.

"Let me tell you something," I said to him, "If I continue with this marriage, I don't want a bunch of promises. I need action! We need to get back to church, talk to someone. This won't happen again."

"I agree!" He said happily.

"I won't ever forget, but I forgive you."

"I understand," he said. "I just want my wife back".

#IAMSECURED

CHAPTER 11

Change is good. Change is necessary.

AFTER THE BOYS AND I returned to Georgia, Karl and I began counseling. The boys went back to school, and we decided to put our oldest on medication for his ADHD. This helped him focus in school and removed stress from me because the strategies we'd been using were not effective. Karl and I were still in search of a church home and one thing Georgia had, were churches. We belonged to a huge mega-church in California, and Karl hadn't been happy there. We agreed to look for a smaller church where people were closer.. We prayed and asked God to find us a little church where we could grow together and our kids could be reared in, something we all desperately needed.

I was in and out of church most of my life, but Karl had never really been in church or didn't know the Bible or God like I did, but he *desired* to, and that was enough for me.

As his wife, I always felt many of our issues could be solved by prayer and seeking God together. He had been through so much he didn't believe in God until he met me. He became curious, and I always prayed for him and it seemed like, the more I prayed, the more he wanted to know. It was not easy, and it definitely wasn't an overnight miracle. I knew he could be saved. We were already young, married, and had children but neither Karl nor I were raised to make church a priority. Now, we were determined to make it one. God had to be the head of our lives because we needed something that no one else could give us, and that was hope, unconditional love, forgiveness, and assurance.

I was working part-time at the boy's school where I met this woman who worked there. We both had kids in the same class and clicked right away. I didn't quite get it, but there was something different about her. She was the first friend I made since moving to Georgia always offered words of wisdom and encouragement and we had a lot in common. One day we were at lunch, and I was telling her about Karl and I looking for a church. I knew she was married and had been born and raised in Georgia. If anyone could point us in the direction of a church, she surely could. To my surprise, she told me she and her husband pastored a church in a city called Smyrna, about twenty minutes away from where we were. It was a small church with a family-like membership. Everyone knew and looked out for each other. I was shocked because this could be the church we'd been praying for. It sounded too good to be true!

I believe there is no such thing as coincidences and God knows who we need. My co-worker and her husband were extremely kind people. They helped Karl and I shortly after knowing us. We'd been having car troubles and couldn't afford to have them fixed and continued to make the best of what we had. The car had no heat or air, often overheated and dropped dead at times. One day, Karl had come to pick me up from work and the passenger door wouldn't close. I went inside and asked for a rope and found a tie to use to hold the door closed. I guess she'd seen us because the next thing we knew, she and her husband were bringing us one of their cars! They didn't ask any questions or ask for any money. They said they saw we were in need, and we could keep the car as long as we needed too. Karl and I knew they were special people and from that day on, we would always look out for them. They had no idea we were struggling in our marriage or finances. They just wanted to help.

The following Sunday, Karl, the boys, and I attended Greater Grace. We didn't have any expectations, and only knew what we'd prayed for needed. When we pulled up, tears formed in my eyes. I grabbed Karl's hand and knew this was the church for us. Karl smiled and wanted to give it a little more time. Afterall, we hadn't actually gone inside yet. The church service was awesome! The members were welcoming and inviting. The boys enjoyed themselves, and when I had a tough time with Kayden, I was offered some help. It was like a dream come true. After service, we had a chance to speak with the First Lady, my co-worker. I hugged and thanked her. I was so happy I couldn't stop smiling.

On our drive home, Karl told me he could see us being members of Greater Grace. Things were finally looking up. A month later we were members, and I received a promotion at work from part-time floater to full-time office staff. I'd become active in church, Karl was part of the men's group, and I'd found a best friend in my First Lady. To add to the abundance, we received the call that we'd been waiting for. The hospital lawsuit had settled, and we flew to California to sign the paperwork. We were overwhelmed and elated at the same time. This was a needed fresh start for us.

#IHAVEPEACE

CHAPTER 12

It Was All A Dream

MOST PEOPLE THINK CHRISTIANS HAVE it easy, but the truth is Christians are tested and tried the most. We are not perfect by any means, but we never give up. Our experiences bring us closer to God, just as they are supposed to. The difference between Christians and non-Christians is our relationship with God sustains us through the tribulations.

It was a sunny Thursday spring afternoon, and I'd arrived at Kayden's doctor appointment for his hearing and vision check. Kayden had survived 10 different procedures and no longer had the feeding tubes in his stomach, and the latest surgery was to remove his feeding tube, but I was still shocked by the results of the visit. Kayden had lost hearing in his left ear and would need tubes placed in his ears. I thought Kayden heard well, but the doctor explained that Kayden was using body language and not words to respond. We scheduled another procedure, and there was no guarantee it would work. Stunned, I went home thinking, "God, we need You again."

I attempted to call Karl. I was eager to share with him the news in hopes of hearing something encouraging from him to keep me from stressing. I called the school to see if Karl had picked up Khalil. When the school said he was still there, I knew something was not right. Karl always picked Khalil up, and he always answered my calls. I rushed to pick Khalil up, and sped home to see Karl's car in the driveway. Before I could get inside, the neighbor ran outside to catch me. She told me an ambulance had come to get my husband. I took a deep breath, ran in the house to change the boys, get them some toys and snacks, and headed back out. Our neighbor told me which hospital they took Karl to. I drove quickly.

I was sweating, hot, and running through the hospital with a backpack full of snacks and toys, carrying one child in my arm and dragging the other going from station to station in the emergency departments asking them if they had my husband. He was being looked at by the doctors and I couldn't see him. He'd passed out and his blood pressure was extremely high. They mentioned the possibility of a stroke. My heart stopped, and I gasped. The next thing I knew, a nurse came from behind the counter and helped me to a seat. She brought me some water, as I sat the kids down next to me in the waiting room. I began to pray. There was nothing else I could do. The events of the day were overwhelming in my mind, but I had to stay calm as I could for Khalil and Kayden.

I wasn't given any details of Karl's condition. I didn't know if he'd be in a wheelchair or come home at all. I wondered if he was being punished for cheating. I thought about how life would be for the boys and me. No matter how much he'd hurt me, I still loved him and I didn't want anything bad to happen. I quickly shook the negative thoughts. Instead, I repeated, "I can do all things through Christ who gives me strength".

I called my family in California. My mom was concerned because we were by ourselves, but I assured her we'd be okay. Although I was certain, I knew whatever God allowed, we'd have the strength to endure. Some hours passed, the boys were restless, hungry, and tired but, I needed to know what was happening with Karl. I was praying more when the nurse returned. I grabbed the boys and headed to the back of the ER. I wanted to prepare myself, but I didn't know what to prepare for. I could only pray it wasn't too bad because I didn't want the boys to see. The nurse knocked on the door of Room 23. We walked through the slightly ajar door, and she pulled back the curtains and there he was.

Karl looked weak in his face with bags under his eyes and grey skin. He managed to open his eyes when we walked in but that was all. Kayden ran to the bed, "Daddy!"

Karl tried to smile.

"Are you in any pain?" Was all I could manage. I sat in the chair next to the bed holding Kayden. He signaled to me to help raise the bed up so he can sit upright. "It's not good," he said as he looked at me with tears in his eyes.

Just then there was a knock at the door and there were two EMT's there with a chart in their hands. The doctor and his nurse quickly followed in behind them. Karl had to be transported to another hospital to undergo surgery. His kidneys had completely shut down, he needed to start dialysis right away and it was a matter of life and death. My mouth dropped. I turned and looked at Karl speechless. The EMT's asked me if I wanted to take his wallet and other personal items home with me. They moved fast! The doctor talked too fast and there was too much happening at once in that tiny room. I had no time to react or begin to process any of it. The only question I could ask was the location of the next hospital. I could tell Karl was angry. He didn't want to be on dialysis, but now there was no choice. I kissed him on his forehead, the EMT's unlocked the wheels on the bed and wheeled him out the doors.

#IAMAMAZING

CHAPTER 13

Money Can't Buy Happiness

THE NEXT SEVERAL MONTHS WERE bittersweet. We built our first dream house, which was a stressful but exciting process. Karl was home adjusting to life on dialysis and being a stay-at-home dad. Kidney failure is no joke. Karl's sole purpose was to be able to provide for his family, and not being able to do that took a toll on him. He went through physical, mental, and emotional changes. We appeared to be doing well to the observer. We loved Greater Grace and our finances were good, and we had everything we'd wanted, but there are some things money can't buy. It can't buy happiness, time, peace of mind, and it damn sure couldn't buy a kidney.

Out of all the responsibilities, the most challenging was encouraging Karl to not give up. Dialysis was hard for him to deal with. He wasn't the same person and became an angry, confused, sad human being who often had thoughts of giving up his life. He was depressed. His strict diet prevented him from eating things he enjoyed. His body was often tired and in pain, not allowing him to do what he wanted. His entire life was turned around, and he didn't know how to deal with it. One day he was fine and the next he had to sit in a chair for four hours daily connected to a machine that took his blood out of his body, cleaned it, and put it back. Karl was afraid of needles and now had to have them in his arm three to five days a week. His energy levels declined, appetite decreased, and the lack of sleep impacted his mental faculties. He was a great stay-at-home dad. He cooked, cleaned, took care of the kids, but hated every bit of it. All the work he put in at home to care for us, still left him feeling helpless, and his pride was wounded. As a man, he wanted to provide for us in a way his body wouldn't allow. His ego and faith were bruised from no longer being able bodied to work. He wasn't ready to accept his situation.

I saw him on the edge of the tub one day. The look of defeat was all over his face and the posture of his body. He had dark circles under his eyes, looked pale and overall, and exhausted. I saw the pain and weariness in his eyes and my heart broke for him.

He looked at me and said, "I can't do this anymore."

I took a deep breath, gathered my strength, and prepared myself to fight this new demon that dwelled within Karl. He was ready to quit.

"I am tired. I don't want to be stuck with needles anymore. I'm not myself, and I don't want to do this."

I pulled up the chair next to him. I looked him eye to eye and pleaded, "Karl I know this is new, and I know your body is tired, but you can't give up now. We need you!"

"You are not in my shoes!" He yelled tearfully. "You are not the one going through this."

"But I am going through it with you!" I yelled back. "We are going through this together, I am right here with you! I am with you. I pray for you, take you to appointments, and wake up each morning with you. This burden isn't yours alone."

He began to pace the floor.

"Karl, we have to believe God is allowing this to happen for a reason. I know it's tough, but we have to hope and believe that He will help us. I believe God will turn this thing around. I won't last forever. It's a test of our faith and I know you don't want to hear this, but He is going to bring you closer to him." I prophesied.

He shook his head. "I don't know."

"You may not understand it now, or even see it, but I trust God. I know you can't hear me now, but I know God got us, Karl."

When I went to hug him, I felt his anger, sadness, and frustration. His hope was fading fast and he felt stuck in a hole with no escape route. His hurt became my hurt, and I made it my duty to be the best caregiver and wife I could be. I refused to accept his death resignation.

We had several more moments like that over the months that followed. Karl's moods continued to fluctuate. The kids and I would stay away from the house on the worst days. I knew it was difficult for him, but I could only take so much before a snap would come. The entire situation brought me closer to God. I had to depend on Him more. I was in a place I'd never been and asked Him for things I would've never imagined. It was one thing as a praying wife to ask God to protect my family and provide for us, but it's another thing to ask God for patience to understand why my husband wanted to kill himself. I asked God to help Karl want to live and provide me the strength to deal with the stress. The stress of Karl not wanting to live. The stress of caregiving. I asked Him to keep my mind regulated through it all. I even asked for a kidney. Those were types of prayers I prayed.

With God's help, I made sure Karl had therapists close to him, and support groups, and I often did it dead tired. I went above and beyond to make sure he was okay. He tried his best to be strong, but I had to be stronger without him knowing. I was committed to my husband, children, and our marriage. I never let him see me cry for him, and never let on how tired and drained I was. I had no choice but to wear my cape day in and day out. I felt like I had no right to complain because I watched Karl get through his suffering each day. If he could do it, I could too. There were brief moments when I would take the cape off, lock myself in the bathroom and cry in the shower. Other days, it would be in my closet during prayer. After, I'd wash my face, smile, grab my cape and continue my day as if nothing was wrong. The help I needed only God could give.

I felt alone, weak, and vulnerable, but I dared not show it. I didn't know anyone who was the caregiver for her children and husband like I was. I knew my strength had to be a superpower that no one would understand but God. I had to dig deep to encourage myself. My family and friends couldn't help. All everyone did was ask how Karl and Kayden were. No one would ever understand. No one could empathize with me, at least that's how it felt.

I watched people go out, have fun, go on vacations, and wished I could too. I desperately needed time for myself, but I didn't have help. Even if I did, my anxiety wouldn't allow me to leave Kayden. Thinking the worst was something I learned from my mother. She was a worrywart who often overreacted. My anxiety started early on in Kayden's life and it just kept getting worse. When I wasn't with him, I worried. Because he was nonverbal, I was afraid someone would hurt him if they got upset and he'd be helpless to tell me. Then, what if something happened to Karl and I wasn't there? I wouldn't be able to live with myself. Vacations and time to myself was appealing, but my purpose was bigger, and my family needed me.

Many times, being a wife and a mother meant my family's needs came before mine and choosing to put myself last was one of the most selfless things I ever did. I'd been spoiled by my parents, former partners, and my husband. I'd always gotten my way, but God humbled me in ways I never could have imagined. My perception of life became that of selflessness. I learned life was not about having everything I wanted, but instead about helping those God placed in my path. I learned that life is about unconditional love and sacrifice. There's nothing wrong with having desires, needs, and success, but what is any of that without humility?

I couldn't be selfish with my life as it was. I couldn't finesse anyone into doing what I desired. I couldn't talk my way out of having children with special needs or an ill husband. I couldn't use money to fix it either. I had to face every diagnosis and situation head on, and it was going to take with all the financial stability, I couldn't get rid of it. When Karl and I wanted to quit, we didn't. That wasn't an option. But what was I to do when I was on the edge of breakdown at every moment? How did I regain control and get back on course? I was weary and had no energy, but I was expected to keep going. It took me a while, but I learned there was only one person who could fix all these things for me and that was God. The more I prayed, the more He sent help.

My help came in the form of my First lady, Savannah. She'd become like a mentor and big sister to me. She taught me what leaning on God truly meant. She poured into me, and I needed that at the time because I always gave at home and had no one to fill me up. I was overwhelmed, but when I was with Savannah, she brought a sense of calm and peace to my life. She and the pastor had been married ten years longer than Karl and me, and she helped me understand marriage better. She helped to learn to rely on the love Karl and I shared to help get us through.

We always had a good time. When we weren't laughing while stuffing our faces and shopping, we did ministry work. Savannah kept me grounded and was the listening ear I never knew I needed. She reminded me that I was never alone and brought a fresh wind in my life, a wind that was much needed. A wind strong enough to rid the dead feelings and old ways of thinking but gentle enough to keep me standing, humble and grateful. I didn't worry and stress as much when we were together. She adored my boys and loved Karl and I without judgement. I opened up to Savannah and allowed her into my world. She understood and was able to help me through difficult situations. On my harder days, she encouraged me. I knew I could trust her.

Freedom to come and go was hard, but Savannah included me in everything she could, even if she just came over and sat on my couch. She always let me know she was there, and I appreciated that. I was amazed by her wisdom and knowledge about life. I wanted to be a better person for myself, family, and others. God had given me what I needed. She was the blessing I prayed for, and as it turns out, the big sister I never knew I needed, and I was glad He'd brought us together.

She introduced me to her friends, who fell in love with me and my family. I was grateful for them all because we didn't have our family in Georgia. They always let us know they were there for us too. We never had kind people around us who were willing to help. It was so foreign to us; I often declined the help even when I needed it because I was used to doing it on my own. Nevertheless, no matter what was going on in our lives, God surrounded us with what and who we needed. My perception of people shifted. I became wiser and stronger. I became more active in church, which became my sacred safe place. At home I was always on edge and anxiety high but at church, with my church family, I felt a sense of relief, and comfort. I could breathe.

I read my Bible more and asked God to help me be more sensitive with Karl as we grow together in Christ. We went to church and prayed more as a couple, and Karl began to accept the way things were. The depression lifted after a few months, and we spent more time than we did in previous months, which is what he'd wanted all this time. He wanted more of me! I wanted more of God, but neither one of us expected our requests to be fulfilled the way they had. We'd learned that prayers were answered in unexpected ways, and our job was to be ready to receive. We learned that life is short, and we needed to expect the unexpected, laugh, and appreciate one another and most importantly, to trust God. Those were lessons no amount of money could buy.

#IAmTheHeadAndNotTheTail

CHAPTER 14

Behind This Smile

RESILIENCE. I CAN SAY WITH some certainty, I'm sick of that! People often compliment me when they learn my story. When they hear Karl's kidney disease journey, Khalil's ADHD, and Kayden's Down Syndrome and Autism struggles, they want to know how I manage to carry it all so well, and how happy I seem and how I have the strength and ability to be willing to help others? I don't mind the compliments or the questions, but let me tell you, there is a lot going on under this cape and behind this smile. But I simply give God the glory when it comes to how I manage, how I do it, how I make it. It's God who gives me strength, hope, and enduring faith. When I'm sick and tired of being resilient and bouncing back, it's God who helps me in my time of need. Resilience is not easy, no matter how it looks. I'm human and there are times I get frustrated, sad and want to run away, but the reality is, I can't. But what I'm learning is to be okay knowing that I won't always be okay. It's okay to not wear my cape all the time. I can take it off and give it to God.

The truth is, I'm a very happy-go-lucky person. I love to help people and get pleasure from making people laugh and smile, even though I'm still learning how to do that for myself. It's easy for me to help others get organized, reach their goals, stay motivated and encouraged because their lives are most likely simpler than mine. I gain fulfillment from helping others because I feel helpless in my own home. Yes, I keep the house together, run between therapy and doctor appointments, go to the grocery stores, I cook and clean, and drive Karl and Kayden to kidney evaluations or doctor's appointments and spend hours at the hospital days at a time. I can do for other people what I can't do for my own family, give them what they need. I can give someone a business idea, business name, find a babysitter for someone, give restaurant recommendations or general life advice, but what I can't give is a kidney to my husband. I can't heal my son from having Down Syndrome or Autism, I couldn't save my son from having ADHD, I pray for them, but I can't heal them. I am not God. I often feel like a failure at times because I don't understand how I can help everyone else and not my own family. On top of all my caregiver duties, I always put myself on the back burner because my reality is I am responsible for the well-being and safety of everyone in my home. I can't change my circumstances, but I can change myself in my circumstances and that is my harsh reality.

How many people take for granted that their kids can walk, talk, get up and go to the restroom, or bathe themselves? We have to do everything for Kayden. Not to mention Kayden fights with us about everything. He is very stubborn and something as simple as changing his clothes can take up to fifteen to twenty minutes because it's always on his time. He likes to move at his own pace, except when we have places to go and things to do and need him to do what we say immediately and not buck against us. It's frustrating. When we discipline him, a meltdown follows. There's a daily cycle of exhaustion, chaos, frustration and anger and it can be very overwhelming. I don't like to complain because through it all we've been blessed and Kayden has everything he wants, but it's hard work. I can't change that, but I can change how I react to it.

I have to suppress anger towards my husband sometimes when I need him because oftentimes after dialysis, or when he does not feel well, he lays down and doesn't move for hours. His body just won't allow it. The house still has to be cleaned, food prepared, diapers still changed, kids fed, clothes washed, and appointments made. When it's time to mow the lawn, clean the dog crate, or miscellaneous tasks, I often end up doing those too. Karl will object saying he was going to do those things, but by the time he does it, I could have done it already. Family pool time is often without Karl now, because the sun drains him. I get upset until I put myself in his shoes. Would I want someone to treat me like this? How must he feel after having all the blood from his body taken out and put back in. I watched him suffer from body cramps and arthritis. He wakes in the middle of the night in pain, and I wake up with him. How could I justify my anger when I knew the toll treatments take on his body? He can't help it.

Karl decided to do dialysis at home, so I turned my office into a mini dialysis center. It sounds selfish, but I had a hard time with that because Karl didn't understand what it meant for me to have him in the comfort of home. I couldn't sleep during treatments. I had to be there if something went wrong. I had to learn emergency preparedness when his machines were alarmed, and what those different alarms meant, and not to mention, make sure he stayed alive while on the machine. I was upset that he would make such a decision without asking for my opinion. People slip into comas, needles fall out of their arms, and they bleed to death, they need a lot of help. I really preferred trained and paid professionals for this job; that's why they have dialysis centers. I wasn't ready for the commitment, but apparently what I felt didn't matter because no matter how much I pleaded with him, he decided he was staying at home. As much as I was against the idea, I would want to be supported in my decision if it were me. Besides, he is the one physically suffering and having to endure the process of dialysis but, when emergencies happen, he calls me. I stayed close, I no longer complained about it, and just let him be while I prayed and asked God to give me patience and understanding. Again, I had to take the cape off and give it to God. The best thing I could do was to accept the things I could not change. I could not change what was happening to him, but I could change how I responded to it. I could change my attitude. I could change my thought process and the more I let go and let God the easier it became.

Karl's health and treatment plan is, not only taking a toll on both of us, but affecting our eldest son, Khalil. He's developed anxiety after watching his father go through kidney failure. Anytime Karl goes to the hospital or doctor, our son freaks out. He's constantly checking on his dad, or he always says "I don't want my dad to die." Even when I leave the house for longer than an hour, he calls to see when I will return. It's heartbreaking, and as much as I pray with him and tell him not to worry, I'm not in his shoes and he has valid reasons to feel concerned. The sad part is, no child should ever have to worry about their parents.

I honestly didn't know it was bad until one day, Khalil's teacher reached out to me offering help. She stated that during class, he'd often say how worried he was about his dad. Initially, I thought he was trying to avoid schoolwork by gaining sympathy. However, his teacher quickly told me Khalil was an excellent student and she never had problems with him. She suggested that I allow him to speak with the school counselors in hopes of helping him cope.

As a mother, I felt helpless and it hurt me to know he was hurting like this. It's my job to protect and help him. If that means speaking with the counselor or finding outside therapy, I was going to do it, and Karl agrees. Anything that will ease Khalil's mind, I am here for. I would be lying if I didn't say the thought of sending all of us to therapy or counseling hadn't crossed my mind. It's so taboo for African Americans to seek help. We are often told to pray and let God fix it. I believe God can do all things, but He also created therapists and counselors for a reason. Mental health is real and as strong as I think I am, I need help too. This is a lot for all of us.

We need a break from reality, but we don't get vacations and it is hitting us hard. When my friends plan trips, cruises, and vacations, I want to be the first to pay my money and confirm I'm going, but the reality is, I can't go, at least not right now. Karl and I have never had a honeymoon or vacationed. We thought after the kids we would be able to travel, that's not easy with Kayden's sensory issues; any noise can cause him to meltdown. A vacation is out of the question when Karl has to be on dialysis four hours a day and having to have all the necessities to ensure his safety. And a vacation is not a vacation when he only has strength to lay down. My husband deserves a vacation just as much as I do, but with his current health status and requirements, it's almost impossible. I envy people who have the freedom to travel. If I find myself getting sad watching or hearing other people have fun, I just remind myself that they deserve breaks too, and if I could I'd have a ball just like them. I can't be sour about other people living their life. I pray one day soon we will be able to take a trip to the beach, or hell, a trip anywhere. A girl's trip sounds really good too. I need time away from my husband, kids, and the worry of making sure everyone else is okay. Karl often tells me I need to go, but how can I? He needs just as much care as the kids; if I leave and something happens to him, I won't forgive myself. I find encouragement in knowing my time will come. It has to, but for now, this is my life. We do what we can in the city as a couple and family.

For my time, I take full advantage of solo grocery runs, and going to the nail shop feels like a vacation. I enjoy every minute of those one to three hour trips. It may sound crazy that I enjoy going to a store, running into Target or Walmart, or picking up some food for the house. I may step out and have dinner with my friends occasionally, but that's it and that's okay for now. It makes me happy because that is truly the only time I have to myself these days. I remind myself that there are mother's out there who don't get the small breaks. I think about starting programs for family caregivers or support groups for us to help one another. No matter what, God always helps me turn my lemons into lemonade, then pour some for others to have. I keep smiling.

Behind my smile, I have lots of pain, stress, anxiety, worry and fears, but I don't wear them, and I refuse to allow them to overtake me. I post motivational and inspirational quotes and words of wisdom on my social media, and people always tell me it's helpful. I let them know I'm happy my post helps them because they encourage me too. I choose to be happy. Happiness is a choice and no matter what my circumstance is, I choose to be happy. I only have one life to live. I can't afford to go through life sad, bitter, depressed or stressed. I chose to be a wife, and I chose to be a mother although I had no idea it would look like this. I didn't choose for the health issues that seem to plague my family, but I do get to choose to be there for them and to live. I choose to help and encourage others, but most importantly, I choose myself. Under the cape and behind the smile, is me, and I must choose her.

#YOUGOTTHIS

CHAPTER 15

The Fight Continues

AS I LOOK BACK OVER the years, I'm amazed at what we've accomplished. We managed to do something that no one else we know has. As the boys grow older, and we wait in anticipation for a kidney transplant, we have learned to accept life for what it is. We learned not to stress over things we have no control of. We learned how to love each other again. We now love one another the way we each need to be loved. We learned patience with one another, and that spread to those outside of our home. We are now able to help others who are experiencing some of the difficulties we did. Karl is a better man, husband, and father. He works full-time, while on dialysis and we still pray for a kidney. I've watched his love for God grow stronger along with his appreciation for me. I made a promise to God when I exchanged vows with Karl. Through thick and thin, good times and bad, through sickness and health until death do us part.

Marriage is not for the weak! No relationship is perfect, in fact marriage is two imperfect people coming together to grow, love and learn. We learned to communicate instead of run. Reader, I encourage you not to give up. Instead, communicate, understand, start over, and be committed. Learning your spouse is never ending, no matter how long you've been married. Karl and I learned how to lean on each other again and most importantly, we remembered to lean on God and His word. Marriage is about commitment, sacrifice, loyalty, and love. Nothing is going to separate us again. We feel unstoppable because we know God has us.

Recently, I was in the bathtub when Karl ran through the door shaking with his phone in his hand looking like he was about to faint.

"This is Duke Hospital! They have a kidney for me!"

I heard what he had said but it wasn't registering with my brain quick enough. This is the call we'd been waiting for! For five years, we tried to imagine this day and it was finally here. I sat up in the tub and said, "Wait, what?"

I was in disbelief. My husband said to the woman on the phone, "Here, talk to my wife" and he hurried and handed it to me.

"Hello?" I said nervously.

The woman on the other line said, "Hello, this is Duke Transplant team and we have a kidney for your husband."

"Are you serious?" I was still in shock.

"Yes!" She said. "You guys need to be here by 7:30 am."

I looked at the phone. It was 9:40pm. Duke University Hospital is in Raleigh, North Carolina. We always tried to have a plan for what to do when we got this call, but I don't think anything can fully prepare us for this day.

"Oh, my God!" I said to the lady on the phone. "Okay we will be there, thank you."

I gave the phone back to Karl so he could finish gathering the information.

I quickly jumped out of the tub, hopped in the shower, and started putting things together in my head. I needed to fly my family to Georgia to take care of the boys for a week while Karl and I were in North Carolina. We'd need them there as soon as possible because Karl and I would take a helicopter to the hospital. Early in 2021, he was accepted into a program called Angel Flight in which pilots volunteer to fly transplant patients to the hospital to get their organ transplant. That was one less thing to worry about. I was going to have one of my babysitters to watch the kids until my family could book the next flight. The problem was, there were no more flights leaving that evening. I quickly had a backup plan. We would pack the kids, take the babysitter, have my friend get the dog, and drive the six hours to Raleigh. The kids and babysitter would be in the hotel two miles from Duke Hospital, while we were at the hospital. I'd get the family on the next flight from California to North Carolina to get the kids and take them back to Georgia.

Everything seemed to be working out and we hit the road at 11pm. I was so tired, I'd been up since 4:00 a.m. and was running on excitement and adrenaline. This was our first road trip in eleven years. Go figure! The roads were empty, and it seemed like we were flying. We called our immediate family and they were all so excited. Khalil is eleven now and he was the first one packed. Kayden is nine and had no clue what was happening.

"This is finally happening." Karl said. He was feeling a plethora of emotions and cried a little. "This is the moment we have been waiting for!" I said. "This is your last night with a bad kidney."

"Man, I know!" He couldn't stop smiling.

We arrived at the hotel at 5:45 in the morning. We got everyone settled in and headed to the hospital. Karl kissed and hugged the boys one last time as a kidney failure patient, and we hopped right back in the car and headed to the hospital. We valet parked the car, got Karl checked in and once inside there was a team of people waiting for him. They welcomed him as they took our temperatures, checked our bags, and pre-screened us. After that, they led us on a five minute walk through the hospital. We went through so many doors I couldn't keep up. So many thoughts were running through my head and all I could do was say "thank the Lord." They sat us down to be registered and finally called Karl back. I got up to walk back with him but was quickly told I couldn't and that I had to leave the hospital because of the pandemic. I wasn't upset, but I thought I'd at least get to walk back with him.

I gave him a final hug. He squeezed me and said, "I got this!"

I kissed him and said, "See you on the other side"

Then he disappeared through the double doors. The nurse told me I'd get calls with updates and to stay nearby so I could see him in recovery. She walked me outside and I waited for the valet. It was now around 7:40am and more people had arrived at the hospital. The valet attendants were extremely busy, so I just sat on this wooden bench next to the valet booth and waited until they brought my car. I didn't mind the wait, in fact, I was so happy and excited it didn't matter how long they took. Karl was finally about to get his kidney. His days of pains and aches, our struggles and fears, all the doctor appointments and hospital trips would soon be over. We could start to live somewhat of a normal life. We could actually travel and enjoy life without worrying about how he was feeling, or if we had enough medical equipment. Khalil could stop worrying, and our anxiety could ease up some. I was grateful our time had finally come and couldn't stop smiling. Just then my phone started ringing. Without looking, I assumed it was my mother who couldn't sleep since she heard the news. She'd been calling us the entire commute from Georgia to North Carolina. I looked down; it was Karl.

This was odd. He should be getting ready to be put to sleep.

"Yes?" I said thinking maybe he just wanted to call me and tell me he loved me before he went under.

"They won't let me get the kidney." He said.

"What?' I said standing up. "What are you talking about?"

"They just gave me a Covid test and said I tested positive for Covid."

I could hear the hurt in his voice.

"No way!" I said. "That is impossible! Tell them to give you another one."

"I told them I feel fine, I don't have any symptoms, I was vaccinated earlier this year. I don't know." He said.

"Put someone on the phone!" I demanded. "Put me on speaker! This is crazy"

I was in total disbelief. "We came all this way for this transplant. We waited five years for this kidney just for you all to say he has Covid?"

Karl was silent. Someone from the team came into the room and started talking to him. I couldn't hear what they were saying, and I was trying to wrap my head around exactly what was going on. I thought to myself "This can't be right." I know Karl wouldn't joke about anything like this. I didn't understand anything that was happening. I slowly sat back down on the bench in a totally different mood and in a new shock.

Karl called back to see where I was, I and told him I was still waiting on the valet.

"I'm getting ready to come down." He said sadly.

Just then the valet attendant brought the car. I threw my things in the back seat and waited in silence. A few moments later a nurse brought Karl down in a wheelchair.

"Good thing you are vaccinated because I would hate to tell someone without being vaccinated that they had Covid."

I just looked at her. "What? He couldn't get the kidney, how is that good?"

"If we would have operated on him with Covid, he could've died, and we won't take that risk" she tried to explain. I just stared.

"You ready?" Karl asked.

"Let's go." We pulled off.

The tears in Karl's eyes broke my heart. He wouldn't allow them to fall down his face but his devastation was evident. September 2, 2021 is a day we'll never forget.

"Damn man, five years" Karl repeated.

I tried my best to stay calm and be optimistic so I wouldn't break down. "Maybe something was wrong with the kidney and God was actually doing us a favor," I said.

He was silent.

"I know this is devastating, but we came this far, and I know your kidney will be here soon. I am so sorry" I said, fighting back tears.

I continued apologizing because I knew how much this meant to him. This could have changed our entire lives, and in less than five minutes, our six-hour trip was over. It wasn't supposed to happen like this. Maybe their test was wrong. I mean, after all, Karl didn't have any symptoms. Covid tests read false positive all the time! I felt horrible moreso; nothing I said or did could change the situation.

We called our family and broke the news, and as expected, they were heart broken. They had questions we couldn't answer. It was overwhelming. We got back to the hotel to tell our son, and his face dropped. He was disappointed and didn't understand. He buried his head in his tablet and sat in a chair in the corner. Karl was taking a call in the hallway, and I tried to explain to Khalil to be strong for Daddy but remembered, he's just a kid. Kids shouldn't have to be strong, worry, or have anxiety about things they couldn't control.

The hotel room was already paid for, and I hadn't slept in over 24 hours, but I didn't want to stay. I went into the hallway to find Karl with his back against the wall and his head tilted up. I walked up to him and hugged him. He put his arms around me and we stood in silence for a moment.

I looked at him and said, "Let's go. There's no reason to stay here. Let's go get breakfast and get back on the road."

He agreed. Karl was handed a very bad hand, but he was trying to be in good spirits. Normally, when you drive somewhere, the trip there seems longer than the return home, but this time going back home, without a new kidney, took forever. I drove while everyone else slept.

I wasn't prepared for any of this. None of us were. Tragedy seemed to be our norm. If it's not one thing, it's another. Our road was the bumpiest, most winding and turbulent one to travel. I know nothing in life worth having is easy, but at what point can we just be okay? None of us asked for this life. Did we do something wrong? Did we not help others enough? Not give back enough? What? What could have been done to change our situation? In what world do people get called for a kidney, drive six hours, go to pre-op, and get told the entire procedure is cancelled? How are we supposed to deal with this? I prayed. "His ways are not our ways, and his thoughts are not our thoughts" *Isaiah 55:8-9* but I would have given anything to understand why this happened.

I'm not saying I lost faith or didn't trust God, but I kept repeating "God knows best" and wondered if I could convince myself that it was true. I know God loves me; I couldn't help but feel my prayers weren't enough for my family. Am I not as faithful as I thought? Was I not pleasing God? Not spending enough time with Him? I prayed for Karl's spiritual and physical healing daily. Was I not doing something right? Why weren't my prayers reaching God? I remembered Jeremiah 29:11, "For I know the plans I have for you said the Lord. Plans to prosper you and not to harm you. Plans to give you hope and a future." God's love is more than any doubt I have. And if there was nothing in this world that I knew, after all we'd been through, why would God just abandon us now? He wouldn't. I couldn't start to let doubt distract me now. I rebuked every negative thought, and I recited all the scriptures I knew by memory.

My drive home was my time with God. It was time for Him to encourage and guide me. To reassure me to trust Him and believe his word. I am a believer, and I knew this was not the end for us. I knew, in my heart, this would be a part of a much bigger story for us. Our faith was being tested because God loves and trusts us enough to know what we can handle. The Bible says "He won't put more on you, than you can bear" *1 Corinthians 10*:3. After all I'd endured in the past ten years, I believe it! No matter what our situation looks like, how hard the struggle is, no matter how much doubt and fear I have, I had to stand firm in knowing that God is Able! I don't know how people make it in this world without God, without God I am nothing! Without faith, I am a dead man walking. If there is nothing else you take away from this chapter just know that "All things are possible to those who believe," Mark 9:23.

We arrived home and went into quarantine since Karl tested positive. We were able to spend quality time and really enjoy the moments we had together. A few days later, we all got tested for Covid, and were all negative. We couldn't believe it. It raised so many questions. This didn't make sense. How was Karl positive a few days prior and now negative? There was nothing we could do, but we did call the hospital to get answers only to be told they had to go by their results. Once again, we were devastated. We had to keep the faith and believe that God had something better. New kidney or not, Karl was still grateful for his life and through the power of prayer, he believed this was not the end for him. He was not ready to give up. I reminded him daily that his kidney was coming, and it would be just right. We would pray and thank God in advance. It was coming. The fight continues.

#IAmdoingmybest

CHAPTER 16

Pray.Inspire.Live

A MONTH PASSED, AND WE were back to business as normal, and never losing faith. We were certain God was going to make us live out our vowels "Through thick and then, till death do us part". Everyone from our church encouraged us and told Karl he was going to have an amazing testimony. My family called daily to check in. We didn't have any new updates but reassured them our time was coming. Until then, I made sure Karl stayed inside as much as possible. We disinfected the house every hour and tried our best to keep him in a bubble just in case we got that call again. We didn't want to take any chances of being devastated again and put ourselves back on lockdown. Karl was on three donor lists. One in Tennessee at Vanderbilt, one for Piedmont in Atlanta, and he was still on the list at Duke. We didn't care where he got the kidney from and were prepared to go anywhere we needed to. All we needed was another opportunity.

One evening Karl and I were saying our prayers and I asked God to bless Karl with a kidney "Right here at Piedmont in Atlanta" I pleaded. I'd never asked God to bless us with a kidney at a certain hospital. After five years of waiting, I figured anywhere we got a kidney from we would be grateful, but after we left North Carolina God reminded me of something. He is a big God and He never does anything small. God can do all things and is the ruler of all things so why not pray for exactly what I wanted? God puts desires in our hearts, and if we desired a kidney thirty minutes away from our home, why would I not ask God for it? We really didn't want to go back to Duke but that was the only hospital that had called. There was one scripture that kept coming to me every single day and that was Matthew 6:26.

"Look at the birds of the air; they do not sow or reap or store away in barns, and yet your heavenly Father feeds them. Are you not much more valuable than they?"

If God makes sure that the birds are full, ants have homes and food, and takes care of the biggest of big and the smallest of smalls, surely, He can provide us with what we need. I believed He could, and He would! From that night on with every prayer, I would ask God to bless Karl with a kidney right here in Atlanta, "Right here at Piedmont."

Karl was skeptical, but I was hopeful. He'd say, "Piedmont never called me for follow ups as much as Duke did".

"You are still on their donor list" I would remind him. "You never know."

A couple weeks later Karl received a call, but it wasn't for a kidney. They asked him to send them a copy of his vaccination card. We'd already received a letter from them letting us know they'd need the documentation for him to stay active on the list. The law requires donors to be fully vaccinated. They couldn't take any risks performing such a major surgery during a global pandemic.

Later on that evening, I was in the tub and Karl walked in the bathroom. I'm never alone just in case you were wondering. He grabbed something and asked about my weekend plans.

"Hopefully dropping you off to get a kidney" I joked.

He smiled, "Man, I know that would be awesome."

I finished my bath and got ready for bed. It was Friday October 15, 2021, around 11:00 pm. I was thinking about re-organizing the boys' closets and going to the gym the next morning. I get up so early on gym days and don't want to wake Karl, so I sleep in the guest room the night before.

It was 6:02am when I heard the guest room door burst open. I sat up thinking I'm going to kill Kayden because he was the only person who woke me up early on Saturdays. I sat up ready to change him and make him some breakfast but to my surprise, it was Karl standing at the door. "Boo!" He called me. "It's Piedmont." He said as he was shaking, ``They have a kidney for me!"

I looked at him for a second. "Wait what? Are you sure?"

"Yes! They are on the phone." He said as he put the phone on speaker. "Here, talk to my wife." "Hello?" I said.

"Yes, this is the Piedmont Transplant Unit. We have a kidney for your husband." The woman's voice was calming.

"Don't play with me." I said to the woman. "Are you serious?"

"Yes." She said, giggling. "He needs to be at the Piedmont Hospital Emergency Room by 8:00am."

It was 6:04am. I threw the covers off and walked towards the bedroom and Karl followed. "Okay." I said, still in shock.

The woman gave Karl all the information he needed and we began making moves. She gave him the address to the hospital and told him not to eat or drink anything. I called a friend to come watch the boys for us. She agreed with no hesitation. Karl was at his sink brushing his teeth and I was putting on my lashes. I dare not go anywhere without my lashes even in emergency situations. We were still in shock as we moved around the bedroom.

"This is nothing but God. This has to be the one for you" I said.

"I pray so." He said.

"Karl?" I called from the bathroom.

"What's up?" He said as he put his hoodie on.

"Let's not call our family until we know for sure this time." I told him.

"Yeah," he said. "I understand."

With what happened only a few weeks prior, I wanted us to be 100% sure this was the kidney for him. I needed to see and know the Covid test results. I needed to see him being wheeled back into the operating room before I told anyone.

My friend had arrived at the house at 7:20am on the dot, excited and happy for us.

"It's funny," she said. "I actually took today off work."

She normally works her part time job on the weekends.

"Oh wow" I said.

"Maybe it's confirmation?" She said.

"Maybe." I agreed.

Karl and I headed out for the thirty-seven minute drive. We were silent for most of the ride. I think we were both nervous about another let down.

"Let's pray" I said as I was getting ready to take the exit. I must have been in a deep prayer because as we were pulling up to the emergency room we were just saying "Amen."

We were greeted by the valet attendant who took the car as we made our way into the building. Just like at the last hospital, they screened us and then proceeded to check Karl in. I took slow deep breaths as I sat and waited. I could hear the women checking Karl in say "Congratulations."

I prayed silently, *Lord, if you be God, this was it.*

We waited thirty minutes before a young lady came and put Karl in the wheelchair. I followed them as she took us through the hospital. There was no one else in sight, it felt like we were the only people there. The halls were bright white, and the hospital looked and smelled clean. The walk from the waiting room to the Transplant Unit seemed forever, but finally we had arrived. There was a big sign that said, "Welcome to the Transplant Unit." It felt so unfamiliar but comforting. I had a good feeling, but I still didn't want to get my hopes up. "If you be God" I said as we walked into Karl's room.

I walked around the room praying quietly.

He looked at me and said, "Can you believe we made it?"

I said "No and I won't until..."

"Until that Covid test comes back?" He finished the sentence for me.

"Yep." I said smiling. "I am so nervous, but I trust God."

Shortly after a slew of nurses filled the room. They explained the next steps and told Karl to shower. The more they spoke, the harder I listened. Everything was happening so fast.

"Do you have any questions?"

I'd been waiting for this moment. "I do! When are you guys going to give him the Covid test?

"The nurse will be coming to do that right after they put his IV in and draw his blood." She explained.

"But if he tests positive what would be the point of taking his blood and starting the IV? I asked. She looked at me puzzled.

"You think he has Covid?" she asked.

"No!" I said too much already. "He had a false positive test a couple months back and wasn't able to get his kidney so I'm a little on edge."

"Oh." She said. "I completely understand, but they will be here shortly."

An hour later, Karl's blood had been drawn and we'd spoken to the doctor, anesthesiologist, and a social worker, but still no Covid test.

"Oh my God," I said to Karl. "When are they taking this test?

I was making him nervous. I just kept saying "God if you be God."

We were both nervous and anxious. Finally, a nurse arrived to administer the test. I never thought I would be happy to see one of those tests in my life. It was a rapid test and results would be quick. I was already nervous and my mom was calling every five minutes. Thirty minutes later, we inquired about the results, but they hadn't come back yet.

Shortly after, a nurse walked in. "They had a cancellation and are ready for you now."

Karl's eyes lit up with excitement.

"Oh wow!" I said standing up to get out of the way.

Two more people came into the room, took the brakes off the bed, and started to wheel him out. "Am I allowed to come down with him? "I asked the nurse.

"Oh yeah," she said. She explained that he would be going back to recovery after the transplant and needed to know where it was. I didn't get a chance to ask her about his Covid results. I just followed behind them back down the long white hallways.

We arrived in the Surgical Unit and Karl was the only person there. The nurses quickly came over and asked him some questions. They then explained that the surgery could take three and a half hours and they don't expect any issues. They gave him his special bonnet to put on, then they asked me to say my final goodbyes, get my hugs and kisses before they took him back.

"Wait." I turned to the nurse who was typing in his chart. "What were his Covid results?"

"Oh, he was fine. It was negative."

I looked at Karl who smiled at me. "Oh, thank you God."

I kissed him through my mask. "I'll see you with your new kidney when you wake up. God is with you."

"This is it Boo."

It was real. I was able to snap a few pictures of Karl before they wheeled him back.

"I love you!" Karl said as he was being pushed through the double doors.

"I love you too." I said with a huge smile.

I watched until he disappeared.

The nurse was so kind as to escort me to the waiting area and just as I hit the door, praise came over me. The spirit hit me, and I had to let out a huge "Thank you Jesus!"

I did a little hallelujah dance. The nurse looked at me like I was crazy "I'm sorry." I said smiling "If you only knew our story."

Without God, nothing seems possible, but with God all things are possible. We only have one life, one chance, one opportunity to do things right because life is not promised. We are not blessed because of what we have, but because He lives in us. My husband and I are still growing in Christ. We still make mistakes and ask for forgiveness every day. We wake up every day thanking God for our imperfect family, and we hope to help other people see life differently from our trials, truths, and testimony.

If you don't know God I invite and encourage you to get to know Him. Seek Him when you are weak. Cry out to him when you are tired. Life is tough but so are we! Never, ever, ever, ever GIVE UP!

#ICANMAKEIT

CHAPTER 17

Affirmations For The Mind Body and Soul

AFFIRMATIONS ARE POSITIVE STATEMENTS THAT can help you to challenge and overcome self-sabotaging and negative thoughts. When you repeat them often, and believe in them, you can start to make positive changes. I repeat affirmations daily! It helps me along with prayer because sometimes we need reminders of who we really are and or who we are trying to be. Repeating affirmations keeps me motivated. If you aren't in a place where you can say them aloud to yourself, then write them down! Do whatever it takes to keep your peace.

Today is the day for change

I choose to be positive

I can overcome negative thoughts

I am worth it

I am courageous

I am thankful

I am successful

I am grateful

I have joy

I am embracing my best self today

I am healthy

I am happy

I am loved

I am brave

I am strong

I have patience

I am radiant

I am chosen

I am not worried

I am powerful

I am intelligent

I am confident

I am well

I am prepared

I am doing my best

I love myself

I forgive myself

I trust myself

I trust my intuition

I am doing my very best

I am proud

I am positive

I am present

I am confident

I am motivated

I am focused

I am empowering

I am at peace

I am rich

I have everything I need

I am the head and not the tail

I am above and not beneath

I am loved

I am influential

I am more than enough

I am beautiful

I am worthy

I can do this

I am appreciative

I am kind

I am rested

I have purpose

I am who God says I am

My heart is full

I can do all things

I am unstoppable

I am amazing

I am okay

I deserve to be happy

Today is a new beginning

I am important

I matter

CHAPTER 18

Scripture List

THIS IS A LIST OF scriptures that I used to help me through the days. Whether I am having a good day or a bad day, these scriptures speak to my heart, they change my mood and keep me humble. Reading over scriptures and repeating affirmations keeps me motivated while striving to be the best me I can be.

Psalm 34:17-19: When the righteous cry for help, the Lord hears and delivers them out of all their troubles. The Lord is near to the brokenhearted and saves the crushed in spirit. Many are the afflictions of the righteous, but the Lord delivers him out of them all.

Psalm 34:17-19: When the righteous cry for help, the Lord hears and delivers them out of all their troubles. The Lord is near to the brokenhearted and saves the crushed in spirit.

Many are the afflictions of the righteous, but the Lord delivers him out of them all.

Psalm 147:3: He heals the brokenhearted and binds up their wounds.

Psalm 55:22: Cast your burden on the Lord, and he will sustain you; he will never permit the righteous to be moved.

Isaiah 41:10: Fear not, for I am with you; be not dismayed, for I am your God; I will strengthen you, I will help you, I will uphold you with my righteous right hand.

Isaiah 40:31: But they who wait for the Lord shall renew their strength; they shall mount up with wings like eagles; they shall run and not be weary; they shall walk and not faint.

Isaiah 42:16: And I will lead the blind in a way that they do not know, in paths that they have not known I will guide them. I will turn the darkness before them into light, the rough places into level ground. These are the things I do, and I do not forsake them.

Jeremiah 29:11: For I know the plans I have for you, declares the Lord, plans for welfare and not for evil, to give you a future and a hope.

Matthew 11:28: Come to me, all who labor and are heavy laden, and I will give you rest.

Romans 8:28: And we know that for those who love God all things work together for good, for those who are called according to his purpose.

1 Corinthians 9:24: Do you not know that in a race all the runners run, but only one receives the prize? So run that you may obtain it.

2 Corinthians 4:8: We are afflicted in every way, but not crushed; perplexed, but not driven to despair; persecuted, but not forsaken; struck down, but not destroyed;

2 Corinthians 5:7: For we walk by faith, not by sight.

Psalm 34:17-19: When the righteous cry for help, the Lord hears and delivers them out of all their troubles. The Lord is near to the brokenhearted and saves the crushed in spirit. Many are the afflictions of the righteous, but the Lord delivers him out of them all.

Psalm 147:3: He heals the brokenhearted and binds up their wounds.

Psalm 55:22: Cast your burden on the Lord, and he will sustain you; he will never permit the righteous to be moved.

Isaiah 41:10: Fear not, for I am with you; be not dismayed, for I am your God; I will strengthen you, I will help you, I will uphold you with my righteous right hand.

Isaiah 40:31: But they who wait for the Lord shall renew their strength; they shall mount up with wings like eagles; they shall run and not be weary; they shall walk and not faint.

Isaiah 42:16: And I will lead the blind in a way that they do not know, in paths that they have not known I will guide them. I will turn the darkness before them into light, the rough places into level ground. These are the things I do, and I do not forsake them.

Jeremiah 29:11: For I know the plans I have for you, declares the Lord, plans for welfare and not for evil, to give you a future and a hope.

Matthew 11:28: Come to me, all who labor and are heavy laden, and I will give you rest.

Romans 8:28: And we know that for those who love God all things work together for good, for those who are called according to his purpose.

1 Corinthians 9:24: Do you not know that in a race all the runners run, but only one receives the prize? So run that you may obtain it.

2 Corinthians 4:8-9: We are afflicted in every way, but not crushed; perplexed, but not driven to despair; persecuted, but not forsaken; struck down, but not destroyed.

2 Corinthians 5:7: For we walk by faith, not by sight.

Galatians 6:9: And let us not grow weary of doing good, for in due season we will reap, if we do not give up.

Philippians 4:19: And my God will supply every need of yours according to his riches in glory in Christ Jesus.

1 Peter 1:6-9: In this you rejoice, though now for a little while, if necessary, you have been grieved by various trials, so that the tested genuineness of your faith—more precious than gold that perishes though it is tested by fire— may be found to result in praise and glory and

honor at the revelation of Jesus Christ. Though you have not seen him, you love him. Though you do not now see him, you believe in him and rejoice with joy that is inexpressible and filled with glory, obtaining the outcome of your faith, the salvation of your souls.

* 9 7 9 8 9 8 5 3 3 4 9 3 7 *